best served cold
the unofficial companion to
revenge

best served cold
the unofficial companion to
revenge

erin balser
ecw press

Published by ECW Press
2120 Queen Street East, Suite 200, Toronto, Ontario, Canada M4E 1E2
416-694-3348 / info@ecwpress.com

LIBRARY AND ARCHIVES CANADA CATALOGUING IN PUBLICATION

Balser, Erin
Best served cold : the unofficial companion to Revenge / Erin Balser.

ISBN 978-1-77041-093-0
ALSO ISSUED AS: 978-1-77090-332-6 (PDF); 978-1-77090-333-3 (EPUB)

1. Revenge (Television program). I. Title.

PN1992.77.R49B34 2012   791.45'72   C2012-905364-3

Editor for the press: Crissy Boylan
Cover design: Rachel Ironstone
Cover image: © Viachaslau Kraskouski / Shutterstock
Thorns: © midnightstouch/brusheezy.com
Photo section images © ABC Photo Archives/ABC via Getty Images.
Printing: United Graphics   5   4   3   2   1

The publication of *Best Served Cold* has been generously supported by the Ontario Arts Council, an agency of the Government of Ontario. We also acknowledge the financial support of the Government of Canada through the Canada Book Fund for our publishing activities, and the contribution of the Government of Ontario through the Ontario Book Publishing Tax Credit. The marketing of this book was made possible with the support of the Ontario Media Development Corporation.

PRINTED AND BOUND IN THE UNITED STATES

introduction

Revenge was supposed to be doomed from the start. It had an over-the-top premise, a melodramatic title, a heavy-handed theme-of-the-week structure, a terrible time slot, and a no-name cast. Its biggest star barely worked in the past decade and its lead had never carried a show. Critics considered the series dead in the water before it even aired.

Then they saw the pilot. The story of a daughter returning to her childhood home to avenge the wrongful imprisonment and eventual death of her father tapped into a collective anger about disparity, inequality, and injustice, as the divide between the rich and poor in North America grows rapidly. Part social commentary and part escapist entertainment, *Revenge*'s mix of traditional soap tropes and TV thriller twists has critics standing up and taking notice. The *Boston Globe* called *Revenge* "a classic guilty pleasure." The *New Yorker* said, "*Revenge* is too juicy to write off as junk." And fans agreed. The *Revenge* premiere won its time slot, with 10 million viewers tuning in. Since then it's been consistently the #1 show at 10 p.m. on Wednesday nights. Slowly, but surely, *Revenge* became the breakout hit of the fall 2011 TV season, leaving viewers scrambling to say "I told you so," Victoria Grayson–style.

Whether it was as simple as keying someone's car or as complex as wanting to destroy someone else's life, we've all dreamed of seeking revenge against someone. (Don't deny it!) We've also dreamed of living an opulent lifestyle, with fast cars, fancy clothes, and fabulous homes. *Revenge* offers us both — but it also shows us that the lifestyle of the rich and infamous isn't all that it's cracked up to be. By vicariously living through Emily Thorne, *Revenge* is simultaneously letting us be the 1% and destroy them. "The reason people are connecting to Emily is because there are so many disenfranchised people, and so many members of the 99% are feeling like somebody else is in control of their futures, of their finances, of the choices that their families are able to make," *Revenge* creator Mike Kelley told the *Daily Beast*. "So when Emily is able to wreak havoc on the people that are the decision-makers, that hold the purse strings, the employers that really seem to live above and beyond the rest of the world, and take those people down, it's wish fulfillment."

Revenge is a fast-paced, complicated, and character-driven show with many plot twists and unanswered questions, and *Best Served Cold* digs deep into it all. I start by going back to ABC's offices and explaining where the concept for the show came from. Then I go back even further and take a detailed look at the original source of inspiration for the show, Alexandre Dumas' seminal novel *The Count of Monte Cristo*. From there, I look at the cast of characters, with portraits of each Hamptons resident and the actor who portrays them on-screen. After that, each episode from season one gets a detailed analysis, focusing on how it reflects the week's titular theme (as pointedly explained by Emily in the voiceover) and how it fits into *Revenge*'s milieu. This is followed by Shamu cam–worthy surveillance of all the extra details, as outlined below:

BEST SERVED COLD Mirror, mirror on the wall, who is the biggest bitch of them all? I'll let you know who wins the crown in each episode and why.

HAMPTONS HOMAGE Mike Kelley digs deep in TV, film, and literary history to build the mythology of *Revenge*. Here I point out the best references to the ghosts of pop culture past.

WHO'S THAT GUY? Lots of famous (and not-so-famous) faces show up on *Revenge*. This is where you find the details on where and when you've seen them.

BORROWED FROM THE BOOK *Revenge* may be "loosely" based on *The Count of Monte Cristo*, but Mike Kelley draws on Alexandre Dumas' classic tale a lot more than he lets on. Here I compare the major plot points found in *Revenge* to those in the book.

BEHIND THE SCENES Sometimes the truth is stranger (or at least more fun!) than fiction. You can find stories from the cast and crew about the making of *Revenge* here.

REVENGENDA Each episode ends up posing more questions than it answers. These are the mysteries that left me wondering as we headed into the next episode.

REVENGESPIRATION Emily Thorne isn't the only one spewing idioms about life, love, and vengeance. I'll highlight the best words of wisdom from the rest of the Hamptonites.

There are a lot of literary references in *Revenge*. And I do mean *a lot*. In the "Revenge Reading" chapters, I explain some of the strongest literary influences seen on the show. It's the perfect place to find your next great read (after *The Count of Monte Cristo*, of course!).

But that's not all. Throughout the book, you'll find explorations of other sources of inspiration for the show and inside information on how the show is made. Just as *Revenge* bounces from past to present, so does this book. So if you're watching for the first time while reading along and don't want to be spoiled, start with the episode guide and work backward. But if you're reading while rewatching, feel free to go from beginning to end.

While I did my best to make this the most badass and comprehensive *Revenge* companion out there, I may have missed a detail or two (Emily Thorne would not approve) or you might not agree with my interpretation of events. And that's okay! Either way, I'd love to hear from you. Email me at embalser@gmail.com.

Don't forget: revenge is a dish best served cold. I hope you're hungry.

— eb

plotting revenge
The Making of ABC's Soaptacular Hit

Revenge opens with a quote from ancient Chinese philosopher Confucius: "Before you embark on a journey of revenge, dig two graves." This sentiment is true not only for those seeking vengeance, but for those developing a TV series. Hundreds of shows are pitched every pilot season. Few are shot. Even fewer are picked up. And even fewer still make it past their first season and become bona fide hits. When *Revenge* was pitched to ABC, it received a lot of support from network executives; Paul Lee, president of the ABC Entertainment Group, admitted the project was one of the network's "internal favorites." But those behind the show — the ABC network, Temple Hill Productions, and Mike Kelley's cast and crew — were cautiously optimistic. They had all buried beloved projects before. But thanks to right team, the right cast, and the right concept at the right time, *Revenge* defied the odds.

While writer and creator Mike Kelley is given a lot of credit for the show (and rightly so) *Revenge*'s journey started long before he came into the picture. It began with the Temple Hill Entertainment team, Marty Bowen and Wyck Godfrey, two producers best known for a series of teen-targeted films about brooding vampires who sparkle.

Before becoming a TV and film producer, Marty Bowen was a talent agent. After graduating from Harvard University, Bowen moved to Los Angeles and landed a job in a talent agency's mailroom. He worked his way up the ladder, eventually becoming a partner at the United Talent Agency. As an agent, he represented some of Hollywood's best and brightest, including *The Sopranos* star James Gandolfini and screenwriter Charlie Kaufman. But after years of finding the right projects for his clients, the Fort Worth, Texas, native wanted to start making his own. "I wanted a creative outlet," Bowen explained to IndianTelevision.com. So he turned to his longtime friend Wyck Godfrey.

By this time, Godfrey had spent 15 years producing films for companies like New Line Cinema. His résumé included *The Mask* (1994), *Dumb and Dumber* (1994), and *Behind Enemy Lines* (2001). The Princeton graduate was ready to develop his own projects when Bowen came calling. In 2006, Bowen and Godfrey both left their jobs and started Temple Hill Entertainment, named after the house they had shared when they were just launching their careers.

The two found success right away with their first film, 2006's *The Nativity Story*. The Jennifer Aniston project *Management* (2008), a modest box-office success, followed. Then Temple Hill decided to bet big on a project that couldn't get off the ground: the film adaptation of Stephenie Meyer's Twilight trilogy. After floundering in development hell for a few years, the project needed producers to breathe life into it again. Director Catherine Hardwicke — who had worked with Bowen and Godfrey on *The Nativity Story* — suggested Temple Hill. They jumped at the chance to bring these books to the big screen, as they saw Temple Hill as a multi-platform company, working on the intersection of books, films, and television. "We stay in those three worlds," Bowen said at the 2011 ContentAsia Summit. "We incubate [ideas] in any of these various mediums." The gamble paid off. The first *Twilight* film (2008) grossed just under $400 million worldwide, launching one of the most successful film franchises since Harry Potter. Bowen and Godfrey — and Temple Hill Entertainment — had arrived.

With *Twilight* red hot, Bowen and Godfrey were eager to keep expanding and started to think about developing projects for television. Creatively, the medium had never been stronger. Patrick Moran, the head of drama development at ABC Studios (and, once upon a time, Godfrey's intern when he worked at New Line Cinema), encouraged Temple Hill to give the small screen a try. In 2010, he offered them a development deal, and Godfrey and Bowen went to work developing two projects for the network: a 14th-century adaptation of Shakespeare's *Romeo and Juliet* and a primetime soap set in the Hamptons.

Bowen and Godfrey chose the Hamptons because they liked the "aspirational element" of the place, Bowen explained. It helped that TV viewers were already familiar with the setting, thanks to shows like *Gossip Girl* and tabloid tales like Diddy's infamous white parties. "We loved the idea of having rich people coming for the summer, interacting with the people who live there the year round," Bowen said. "We thought that there was really interesting drama to explore."

ABC agreed but thought the idea needed further development. So Temple Hill turned to literature for inspiration. Their first idea was a modern-day adaptation of F. Scott Fitzgerald's *The Great Gatsby*. "[It] was a step in the right direction," Bowen said, but they decided the *Gatsby* concept simply wasn't suited to serial storytelling. They tossed around a few more ideas and eventually landed on *The Count of Monte Cristo*. It wasn't the winner right away, but as Bowen and Godfrey went through more and more books and concepts, they found themselves coming back to Alexandre Dumas' classic tale of revenge. It "just stuck" and they took the idea to ABC.

The network liked the concept but asked for one major change: they wanted the story told from a female perspective. Bowen and Godfrey agreed. Thanks to *Twilight* and their film adaptation of *Dear John* in 2010, Temple Hill already had success with female-oriented storytelling and thought the network's suggestion played to their strengths as a production company.

The show's title came next. Paul Lee can take credit for that. The show would be called *Revenge*.

They had a setting, they had a hook, and they had a name, but they needed a visionary to bring it all together. That's when Mike Kelley came aboard.

Mike Kelley, born in 1967, grew up in the sleepy suburban town of Winnetka, Illinois. He landed his first TV gig in 1999, co-writing episodes of the NBC drama *Providence*. When *Providence* was abruptly canceled in 2002, Kelley went to work on The WB teen drama *One Tree Hill*. While primarily a writer for his two seasons there, Kelley gained some producer experience before leaving in 2005 to write for the biggest teen drama of the decade: *The O.C.* It was on that set that his boss (presumably TV producer Robert De Laurentiis, who worked with Kelley on both shows) gave him some advice that changed the course of Kelley's career. "It was one thing to write other peoples' scripts," Kelley recalled his boss saying to Chicagoist.com, "but you should really challenge yourself to do something that's personal to you, that has your own voice, before you get stuck in the rut of doing other people's shows." So Kelley quit, and he began developing something that would be wholly his own: a subversive series set in the 1970s called *Swingtown*.

Pitched as *Boogie Nights* meets *The Wonder Years* to potential TV networks, *Swingtown* looked at middle-class couples living in suburban Chicago as they dealt with the social and sexual changes that were shaking up America at the time. The show was originally intended for cable, thanks to its explicit sex, drug use, and swearing, but CBS decided to take a chance on Mike Kelley's script and ordered a 13-episode run. *Swingtown* premiered in June 2008 and was warmly received by critics, but it didn't turn on audiences. Midway through the series' run, CBS quietly moved it to Friday nights (a death knell in TV land) and, when it was finally canceled at the end of the year, no one was surprised.

The show failed, but CBS was impressed with Kelley. They offered him a two-year, seven-figure development deal. His first project under this deal was a drama starring Sean Hayes called *BiCoastal*. When that fell through, CBS asked Kelley to step in as the showrunner for *The Beautiful Life: TBL*, created by Ashton Kutcher and former *Swingtown* writer Adam Giaudrone and starring *The O.C.* actress Mischa Barton. Despite early buzz, *TBL* failed to find an audience and "died a merciful quick death," Kelley said, when it was canceled after two episodes. Kelley completed his final project for CBS — a 2010 pilot called *The Quinn-tuplets* that was never picked up — before

Emily VanCamp with the men of *Revenge*:
(L to R) Josh Bowman, Mike Kelley, Gabriel Mann, and Nick Wechsler.

parting ways with the network. "I wanted to hook up with a network that was a better fit for my sensibilities," he told *Deadline Hollywood*. And with that, Kelley was left to figure out his next move.

When ABC and Temple Hill heard that Kelley was free and looking, they jumped at the chance to meet with him. "We were fans," Bowen admitted. "I saw how good his writing was and how good [*Swingtown*] was." Kelley felt good about the meeting and liked the *Revenge* project. But he had one concern: *The Count of Monte Cristo* spans 20 years and has dozens of characters. He felt that a straightforward, linear narrative wouldn't do the story justice. So Kelley made a suggestion that would define the show: "My take on it was to do it through the eyes of a wronged child and have her come back for revenge." Bowen, Godfrey, and the network said yes. From there, the project and the partnership came together quickly, and ABC signed Kelley to write the pilot and run the show.

With Kelley in place, the team began looking for a director for the pilot, and they found a perfect match in Phillip Noyce. Known equally for box-office blockbusters and acclaimed independent films, Noyce is a versatile and respected director. Born in New South Wales, Australia, he studied at the Australian Film, Television and Radio School and made several award-winning short films before he transitioned into full-length features. *Backroads* (1977) and *Newsfront* (1978) brought him success in Australia before he decided to move to Los Angeles. His first Hollywood film, the 1989 thriller *Dead Calm*, made Nicole Kidman a star. The box office smashes *Patriot Games* (1992) and *Clear and Present Danger* (1994), both based on Tom Clancy novels and starring Harrison Ford, followed. After 1999's *The Bone Collector*, Noyce decided to take a break from Hollywood and seek out new kinds of projects. "If anyone ever writes a summary of my work, I hope they call me a chameleon, because they'd find it totally impossible to categorize me, at least stylistically," he said in *A Cut Above: 50 Film Directors Talk About Their Craft*. He returned to Australia to make *Rabbit-Proof Fence* (2002) and *The Quiet American* (2002). Both films garnered Noyce several awards for directing in Australia and America, and *The Quiet American*'s star, Michael Caine, earned an Oscar nod. Noyce returned to big-budget films in 2010 when he directed *Salt*, reuniting with *The Bone Collector* star Angelina Jolie.

Even though Noyce is best known for his films, he's no stranger to television. His TV credits included *Tru Calling* (2003), *Brotherhood* (2006–2007), *Lights Out* (2011), and *Luck* (2012) by the time ABC approached him to direct the *Revenge* pilot. ABC signing Noyce was part of a larger trend of feature film directors doing

Phillip Noyce on set of the pilot episode of *Revenge*.
(COURTESY OF MARCI PHILLIPS, FISHY FISHY CAFÉ)

television; at least 10 pilots were directed or produced by film directors for the fall 2011 season. ABC, Temple Hill, and Kelley wanted Noyce because of his consistent delivery of high-quality projects. He also had a knack for working on projects built around strong female characters, making him the perfect person to take Kelley's script from page to screen. Known for being demanding and detail-oriented, Noyce brought this eye for excellence to every step of *Revenge*'s development, from casting to the pilot's final cut. Every scene in *Revenge*'s pilot was mapped out before a single second of film was shot. It's this thorough and rigorous process that makes so many of his projects a success. "Phillip is very demanding," Kelley told the *Sydney Morning Herald*. "He challenges me to answer every possible question he can think of — and he thinks of a lot."

With the creative team in place, it was time to find the cast. The team knew that they needed the perfect actress for the role of Emily Thorne, someone who could walk the line between girl-next-door charm and sociopathic determination. Emily VanCamp, who had recently left the TV show *Brothers & Sisters* because she wanted more creatively fulfilling work, was mentioned as a possibility, and the script was sent her way.

ABC was familiar with VanCamp, thanks to *Brothers & Sisters*, but they weren't sure if the Canadian actress, who had built her career on playing good girls, could handle such a dark and complex character. With these reservations in mind, Kelley and his team took a meeting with her. Kelley immediately wanted VanCamp to play Emily Thorne. "You look at her and you see the girl next door, your first girlfriend, or your friend's niece," Kelley said to *Flare*. "You don't think of her as somebody that's going to be bent on revenge." But ABC still wasn't ready to commit and asked VanCamp to go through an audition process. After her first screen test, she didn't hear anything about the part for over a month. Then out of the blue ABC called her and wanted her to do a second screen test — right away. She came in and "killed it," according to Kelley, and the part was hers.

The casting process was a bit easier for the role of Victoria Grayson. Kelley knew that the actress who would fill those sky-high Louboutins had to be formidable but also had to have class, grace, and nuance. It had to be someone like Madeleine Stowe. "You just don't forget her," Kelley told the *Los Angeles Times*. But they never dreamed she'd be interested in the part — until she called. Stowe had read the script and wanted a meeting. Kelley and Bowen were thrilled to hear from the former film actress, and it wasn't long before they secured their second star for *Revenge*. "We loved her," Kelley told the *Futon Critic*. "She brings complexity and craft and a feature credibility that I can't imagine the show without. We got very lucky!"

After their two stars signed on the dotted line, the rest of the cast fell into place. Phillip Noyce convinced Henry Czerny (Conrad Grayson) to join the project. Noyce knew Czerny from *Clear and Present Danger*, the actor played CIA deputy director Robert Ritter. Ashley Madekwe (Ashley Davenport) had worked with Mike Kelley on *The Beautiful Life*. He sent her the *Revenge* script, complete with a British character named Ashley, and Madekwe knew the part was hers. As for the rest of the *Revenge* cast — Gabriel Mann (Nolan Ross), Josh Bowman (Daniel Grayson), Christa B. Allen (Charlotte Grayson), Nick Wechsler (Jack Porter), and Connor Paolo (Declan Porter) — well, they got their parts the old-fashioned way: they auditioned for them. Bowman believes he was cast because he "had the right preppy look." Mann stood out because when he saw in the script that Nolan was a bad dresser, he put on every terrible piece of clothing in his closet. "I put on a red windbreaker and every other ugly, ill-fitting thing I could dig out," Mann told the *New York Times*.

The cast and crew went to work. They spent 11 days in North Carolina, creating the world that would become Emily Thorne's. ABC liked what they saw and gave the show a 13-episode order and a fall 2011 premiere. Kelley — who at this point was now primarily responsible for *Revenge*'s creative vision — chose to approach the first 13 episodes by telling a self-contained story. That way, if the show was canceled, fans wouldn't be left hanging.

A strong marketing push from ABC helped *Revenge* to a solid premiere on September 21, 2011, and it wasn't long before ABC ordered a full-season pick-up. While many network television dramas have 24 episodes in a single season, *Revenge* got only 22. This is exactly what Kelley wanted, so he could create a tightly written story that could satisfy the show's fans without getting in over his head. "It's a really, really complicated show," Kelley said to the *Hollywood Reporter*. "I didn't have any idea, frankly, when I jumped into this how complicated the serialized nature of this can get."

Kelley took the same self-contained approach to the second half of the season, wanting to tell a complex, creatively satisfying story that could open up other plot lines if *Revenge* was picked up for a second season. "At the end of [season one], I think people will feel that a very significant book of *Revenge* has been written," Kelley told *TV Guide*. "It will free us up to do another book next season." It worked: a single scene in the season finale wrapped up several storylines while setting up the second season in a way no one expected.

With the first season (somewhat) closing one chapter of Emily's story, Kelley has his eye on the future. He's confident that *Revenge* can continue indefinitely. "I wanted to know that I could extend the life of *Revenge* to be a satisfying series, and if I didn't think I could do that, I wouldn't have taken on the series," he told the *New York Post*. "We have so many places [left] to go." While Kelley is still working out the specifics, he knows exactly how Emily's journey ends. "The only way out of revenge," he said, "is either demise or forgiveness, so that's where we're ultimately headed."

Hang on for a wild ride.

REVENGE REWIND
MUST-SEE TV

Movies, literature, television: *Revenge* borrows from them all. The series may be the twisted love child of *The Count of Monte Cristo* and *Dynasty*, but it also owes quite a bit to many other television shows that have come and gone over the years. Below are six must-see shows if you want to understand the television traditions *Revenge* honors.

Dallas (1978–1991): The entire soap genre should be thanking *Dallas*. The original primetime soap followed greedy oil baron J.R. Ewing and his dysfunctional family through 14 seasons of highs and lows. Money, love, sex, and power were the driving forces of many of the show's plot lines. *Dallas* introduced many now-common soap storylines to primetime, including mysterious murders (the infamous "Who shot J.R.?" storyline resulted in one of the most-watched TV episodes of all time), an entire season that turned out to be a dream, and gripping season-ending cliffhangers. *Dallas* also set the tone and visual style for future soaps, including *Revenge*: campy, glamorous, indulgent, and over the top. The *Revenge*/*Dallas* relationship is proof that what goes around comes around, as *Revenge*'s success may have contributed to the greenlighting of the TBS *Dallas* reboot, which premiered in the spring of 2012.

Dynasty (1981–1989): *Dynasty* was ABC's answer to CBS's *Dallas*. It moved the drama from Texas to Colorado, upped the glamour quotient, and cranked out storylines at a breakneck speed (something *Revenge* does today). But the basic premise remained the same. *Dynasty* brought shoulder pads to soaps and Joan Collins' Alexis Carrington, a conniving, damaged ex-wife who birthed a thousand imitations and homages on future television shows, including *Revenge*'s grand dame Victoria Grayson.

***Knots Landing* (1979–1993):** Set in a fictional affluent suburb of Los Angeles, *Knots Landing*, a spin-off of *Dallas*, eventually drifted away from its origin series and outlasted the show to which it owed its existence. While other soaps explored sprawling multi-generational families, *Knots Landing* originally put a microscope on four couples connected by sharing a street address, not a last name. Many of the power plays, victories, and defeats negotiated between these couples became the template for TV marriages of the future, including Victoria and Conrad's.

***The O.C.* (2003–2007):** *Revenge* creator Mike Kelley got much of his primetime soap training as a staff writer for the Fox drama about wealthy families in Orange County, California. Wealthy kids running amok, wealthy parents too caught up in their own problems to notice, and high-octane drama for both generations? Swap coasts and ignore that pesky vengeance plot line and *Revenge* sounds a whole lot like *The O.C.* Blending teen TV with traditional soaps — deaths, births, weddings, divorces, drug and alcohol abuse, sex, lies, and betrayal all made regular pit-stops in Newport Beach — *The O.C.* moved along at warp speed and wrapped it all up in a glossy bow. Its success opened the door to the next generation of primetime soaps.

***Desperate Housewives* (2004–2012):** *Revenge* has *Desperate Housewives* to thank for bringing the soap genre back to ABC primetime. While the once-hot *O.C.* fizzled after four seasons, everyone's favorite fictional housewives held strong for twice that time. The story of four women whose seemingly perfect lives are filled with secrets, lies, and murder wasn't a return to the full-on evening soap of the '80s, but the series' popularity showed that modern audiences were receptive to serial storytelling (complete with dramatic voiceover). Thanks to *Desperate Housewives*, ABC was willing to take a risk on a show with a strong premise and intriguing characters, a show like *Revenge*.

Lost (2004–2010): Okay, *Lost* is not a soap. It's not even close. But *Revenge* owes a lot to this critically acclaimed cult favorite. Mysterious plane crashes, flashbacks that propel plots forward, an island setting, an ever-deepening mythology, and captivating characters in need of redemption who constantly keep you guessing: both shows have all this and more. As *Revenge* sped toward the season one finale, even more *Lost*-type elements came into play. Viewers were left asking more questions as the show's puzzling conspiracies developed and, like with *Lost*, the fun of figuring out what is going on lies ahead for *Revenge* fans.

the origin story

Alexandre Dumas' *The Count of Monte Cristo*

No piece of literature has captured the classic story of revenge as artfully or engagingly as Alexandre Dumas' 1844 novel *The Count of Monte Cristo*. As *Revenge* progresses, it spirals away from the details of its original source of inspiration, but Dumas' themes of justice, hope, loyalty, and faith remain constant throughout Emily Thorne's journey.

Alexandre Dumas, who was born into an impoverished family in 1802 in rural France and moved to Paris at 19, was a prolific and accomplished writer. He's best known for writing *The Count of Monte Cristo* and *The Three Musketeers*. Like many stories written during that time period, *The Count of Monte Cristo* was originally serialized. Weekly installments appeared in France's *Journal des Débats*. While it received mixed reviews when it was first published, *The Count of Monte Cristo* is now considered one of the greatest works in Western literature, with numerous film, television, and stage adaptations. And its reach extends beyond artistic endeavors: there's a gold mine, a sandwich, and even a line of cigars named after Dumas' story.

As talented as he was, Dumas can't take all the credit for *The Count of Monte Cristo*. Author Auguste Maquet — a frequent Dumas collaborator

— is responsible for outlining the novel. And the book is actually inspired by a real-life tale of revenge. According to several sources, it all began in 1807 with a man named François Piçaud. Piçaud was engaged to marry a wealthy woman. His friends were jealous and framed him for a crime he didn't commit. When he was in prison, Piçaud met a rich man who left him his fortune; upon his release, he returned to his hometown and sought revenge against those who had framed him.

Dumas' version takes place in 1815 and follows Edmond Dantès, a young man who seems to have it all. He's in love with a beautiful woman, Mercédès; has an adoring father; and has just landed his dream job, captaining a ship. Just as in Piçaud's real-life tale, Dantès' success upsets his so-called friends: Fernand Mondego is jealous of Dantès' relationship with Mercédès; neighbor Gaspard Caderousse resents Dantès' financial well-being and rising social status; and Danglars envies Dantès' career.

When these "friends" learn that Dantès was asked to deliver an incriminating letter to someone in Paris (unbeknownst to good-hearted and naïve Dantès, who was just honoring a friend's request), they decide to use this as an opportunity to frame Dantès for treason. It works. Dantès is found guilty and sent to jail. There, he meets a priest named Abbé Faria, a fellow prisoner. Faria befriends Dantès, informs him of treasure on the island of Monte Cristo, and teaches him about culture, art, and combat. After 14 years of imprisonment, Dantès escapes, hunts down this fortune, reinvents himself as the Count of Monte Cristo, and makes it his life's mission to destroy the lives of those who destroyed him.

Revenge has the same basic premise as *The Count of Monte Cristo*: someone who was wronged many years ago returns under a new identity, infiltrates a prestigious community, and secretly works to ruin the lives of their enemies. But the similarities don't end there. Moments, themes, and characters, big and small, found their way from 19th-century Marseille to the modern-day Hamptons, thanks to Mike Kelley's skillful storytelling.

THE COUNT OF MONTE CRISTO
CHEAT SHEET

If you haven't read *The Count of Monte Cristo* (and I highly recommend it!), here's a cheat sheet to the important characters to help you make comparisons while watching *Revenge*:

THE DANTÈS

Edmond Dantès: A sailor who is wrongly convicted of treason. He eventually escapes prison and comes back, disguised as the Count of Monte Cristo, to seek revenge against those who framed him.

Louis Dantès: Edmond's loving and supportive father. After Dantès is sent to prison, he's so upset that he refuses to eat until Dantès returns, and he dies of starvation.

DANTÈS' ALLIES

Abbé Faria: A priest and fellow prisoner. He is Dantès' mentor and educator and is the one who tells him about the fortune on the island of Monte Cristo. When Faria dies, Dantès hides inside the body bag to escape prison.

Jacopo: Dantès' shipmate and friend, who he meets after escaping from prison.

Giovanni Bertuccio: The Count's faithful assistant. He's loyal to Dantès, and Dantès uses him for information. Bertuccio has his own vendetta against Villefort, which is why he aligns himself with the Count.

THE MORRELS

Monsieur Morrel: A shipbuilder and owner, he awards Dantès his captainship. After Dantès is imprisoned, Morrel is very generous to Dantès' father and firmly believes Dantès is innocent. While Dantès is in prison, Morrel loses his fortune; upon Dantès' release, he repays Morrel for his generosity by anonymously restoring it.

Maximilian Morrel: Monsieur Morrel's son, who is devoted to his father and their business. He falls in love with Monsieur Villefort's daughter, Valentine.

Julie Morrel Hebault: Monsiuer Morrel's daughter, who is the happiest, most satisfied person Dantès meets throughout his journey, despite the fact her family is poor and publicly scorned.

DANTÈS' ENEMIES

Gaspard Caderousse: Dantès' jealous neighbor who agrees to go along with Danglars' plan. Caderousse is given the opportunity to redeem himself by Dantès, but fails.

THE DE MORCEFS

Fernand Mondego: A fisherman who loves Mercédès and helps frame Dantès for a chance to be with her. He later goes on to have much personal and financial success and is named the Count de Morcerf.

Mercédès Herrera: Dantès' fiancée. Once Dantès is sent to jail, Mercédès marries Fernand, but her heart always belongs to Dantès.

Albert de Morcerf: Mercédès and Fernand's son. Dantès originally believes he is spoiled and egotistical but learns he is kind, well meaning, and goodhearted.

THE DANGLARS

Baron Danglars: A financier who becomes extremely wealthy, he comes up with the plan to frame Dantès. Dantès uses his greed to ultimately destroy him.

Madame Danglars: The baron's wife. She is having an affair and selling information she gets from her lover. She also had an affair with Monsieur Villefort that resulted in an illegitimate child, Benedetto.

THE VILLEFORTS

Monsieur Villefort: An ambitious prosecutor. He believes that Dantès is innocent, but goes along with framing him in order to protect his own family.

Madame Villefort: Valentine's stepmother. Viciously protective of her son and his future, she tries to murder her stepdaughter.

Valentine de Villefort: Monsieur Villefort's daughter with his first wife. She is set to inherit her grandfather's fortune and for this reason is hated by her stepmother.

Édouard de Villefort: The son of Madame and Monsiuer Villefort and Valentine's younger half-brother. His mother adores him and does everything she can to protect him and his future.

Benedetto: Madame Danglars and Monsieur Villefort's illegitimate child, who was rescued by Bertuccio shortly after being abandoned by Villefort and raised as someone else's child.

In *The Count of Monte Cristo*, Dantès is framed and loses everything. In *Revenge*, it is David Clarke. But instead of having the same character return for vengeance, as Dantès does in *Monte Cristo*, in *Revenge*, Emily Thorne does the dirty work. While Emily's return to the Hamptons is about avenging her father, it's also about seeking retribution for herself. She suffered just as her father did. As David wasted away in prison, she wasted away in foster care and juvenile detention, suffering, watching, and waiting — just as Dantès did. This change — having two characters split Dantès' journey — allows *Revenge* to explore the familiar story in new ways: it emphasizes how the actions of one person affects many (a theme we see repeatedly in the series) and it opens up the possibility of new storylines and conflicts as Emily learns the truth about what happened to her father.

While David's character and journey is drawn from Dantès' downfall, Emily's is based on who Dantès becomes. Both Dantès and Emily are well educated and receive rigorous training from their mentors. Both come into unexpected wealth thanks to the giving and loyal nature of someone they hardly know. Both adopt new names and identities that signify wealth and high social status, and they buy lavish houses designed to impress their neighbors and attract attention. Both believe that the worst possible punishment for their enemies isn't death, but relentless suffering. Both are singularly focused, cold-hearted, and value one thing above all else: revenge.

Several of the takedowns on *Revenge* are based directly on those in *The Count of Monte Cristo*: Dantès destroys a financier by using his pecuniary greed against him (reimagined as Emily's takedown of hedge fund manager Bill Harmon); Dantès destroys an ambitious attorney-turned-politician by revealing his affair and illegitimate child (reimagined as

Emily's takedown of Senator Tom Kingsly); and Dantès destroys his social-climbing neighbor by using his desire for money and social standing against him (reimagined as Emily's takedown of Lydia Davis). Dantès spends years planning and executing his plans, but Emily? Give her a few days. Getting these takedowns out of the way early in the series reduced the number of characters the show had to juggle (it's easier to follow dozens of people over 1,300 pages and 20 years than it is through an hour of television a week) while also quickly establishing to the audience at home that Emily Thorne means business.

Besides, we don't need a cast of thousands when we have Victoria and Conrad Grayson.

Victoria is primarily modeled on Mercédès, Dantès' fiancée, but she also takes on attributes of the other women involved in the conspiracy against Dantès. Like Mercédès, Victoria watches the man she loves punished unjustly and spends years pining for him. And, like Mercédès, Victoria eventually chooses to honor him rather than continue to live a lie. Like prosecutor Monsieur Villefort's wife, Madame Villefort, Victoria has an unhealthy obsession with her son. And like financier Baron Danglars' wife, Madame Danglars, Victoria is in a marriage largely for the financial and social benefits. Both women turn to other men to find happiness and end up bearing an illegitimate child.

Dumas' female characters become involved in the conspiracy thanks to their husbands, but each remains responsible for her own actions. Though Victoria Grayson exists nearly two centuries after these women, she's in a very similar position: first and foremost, she's Conrad Grayson's wife. For these women — Victoria included — their social status is all they have; without independent means, they use it to provide for the ones they love and to give themselves a sense of worth and purpose. They'll do anything to protect that. The difference lies in that Victoria pursued this lifestyle while the female characters of *The Count of Monte Cristo* were born into it. Victoria's choice to follow in the footsteps of Dumas' women reinforces the idea that this story is a classic one — and demonstrates that women still have a long ways to go in the fight for equality.

This commentary on gender makes the fact that *Revenge* chose to make their protagonist a woman all the more interesting. The expectations placed on a single, wealthy young woman in 2011 are far different from those placed on a wealthy, middle-aged man in the 1800s, giving *Revenge* the space to make this story truly its own.

Just as Victoria reflects the women who betrayed Dantès, Conrad is modeled on the men. Like Fernand Mondego, he watches the woman he loves yearn for someone else. Like Monsieur Villefort, he wants to protect his family and career. And like Baron Danglars, Conrad just likes winning — at his job, at games, and at life. Henry Czerny believes that Conrad's intention is "to remain in a position regardless of what seems to be going on; to be able to, if push comes to shove, just go somewhere; to have the means to always be able to free himself from the comings and goings that I think he on some level enjoys." The same can be said for Fernand, Monsieur Villefort, and Baron Danglars. Each lives under expectations placed on them by their wives, their families, their employers, and their social status. And they accept those expectations and strive to live up to them. In *The Count of Monte Cristo*, the women's journeys are defined by their relationships — with their children (Villefort), their lovers (Danglars), or both (Mercédès) — and the men's journeys are defined by the wealth they've built for themselves — their career (Villefort), their fortune (Danglars), or their title (Fernand). The same is also true for Conrad and Victoria: as Emily's plot against them plays out, Conrad concentrates on saving his company, while Victoria concentrates on saving her relationships with her children.

Dantès' nemeses have children: Albert (the son of Fernand and Mercédès) and Valentine (the daughter of Monsieur Villefort and the stepdaughter of Madame Villefort). Daniel's story parallels Albert's: Dantès originally sees Albert as fair game and uses him to get closer to his parents. However, as Dantès gets to know Albert better, he realizes that Albert is a good person trying to be more than his title and last name. Charlotte's story parallels Valentine's: Valentine is largely ignored by her family and loathed by her stepmother who constantly tries to undermine Valentine in an effort to protect her son's inheritance.

Valentine eventually finds happiness in her relationship with Maximilian Morrel, the poor shipowner's son, much to the dismay of her family.

What Albert and Valentine, and Daniel and Charlotte, demonstrate is that it's too simple to categorize someone as evil and assume everyone and everything associated with them is also evil, simply by sharing a name, a home, or DNA. Justice and morality are complicated and messy — even more so when feelings are involved. Which, of course, makes exacting revenge that much more difficult, and that much more entertaining to watch.

Both Dantès' and Emily's plans are further complicated by the presence of good-hearted, faithful people who believe in doing the right thing: the ship-owning Morrels and the bar-owning Porters. The Morrels are a once prosperous, now poor family who Dante used to work for. Like the Morrels, the Porters provide an interesting contrast to the rest of the characters. What they lack in monetary assets, they make up in loyalty, faith, and love. They aren't swayed by money, status, or power. Monsieur Morrel believes in Dantès' innocence and takes care of Dantès' father while Dantès is in prison. Jack does the same: he stood by Amanda, believing she was out there and deserving of happiness, and he gave Sammy a home. Morrel's daughter, Julie, is in a happy, satisfying relationship; she and her husband want for nothing because they believe that as long as they have love and family, they have everything they need. The same is true for the Porters: it is Carl Porter's goal to keep them together and their bar afloat no matter what. As long as they have each other, everything will work out. This goodness makes Dantès and Emily question their nefarious plans. Is a life solely dedicated to revenge worth living?

Even though Nolan Ross is in a (very) different tax bracket, he also represents the Morrel line of thinking. Like Monsieur Morrel with Dantès, Nolan remained kind and faithful to David Clarke until the very end. And like Dantès' shipmate Jacopo, Nolan remains loyal to Emily, no matter how dark and dirty her schemes get, all while providing a voice of reason (that is often ignored). Dantès finds Jacopo annoying, just as Emily finds Nolan bothersome. In the 2002 Kevin Reynolds–directed film adaptation of *The Count of Monte Cristo* (wherein much of the plot was changed or condensed from the original text, but the themes and heart of the story remain very much the same), Jacopo is always game for vengeance, but he doesn't want Dantès to lose sight of what really matters. Just as Jacopo tells Dantès to "take the gold, take the woman, and live your life! Stop this plan, take what you have won!," Nolan tells Emily to "go make little volunteer babies" with Jack in "Chaos." Emily and Dantès lost the lives they knew, but they haven't lost the right or ability to rebuild a new life, to live fully and happily.

Nolan is also like Bertuccio, Dantès' loyal assistant. Dantès repeatedly uses Bertuccio to gain information about his targets, and it's unclear why Bertuccio is willing to be taken advantage of in this way — until it's revealed that Bertuccio wants to avenge his brother, who was killed at the hand of Villefort. Nolan has his own mysterious reasons for helping Emily, and as much as he's similar to Jacopo, he's more than a faithful sidekick and a voice of reason. He has plans of his own, which include protecting his aunt Carole — and who knows what else.

In *The Count of Monte Cristo*, the Morrels, Mercédès, Alfred, and Valentine eventually get the happy endings they deserve, while the Villeforts, the Danglars, and Fernand get what is coming to them. But the book has yet to be written on *Revenge*; what will become of Jack, Declan, Conrad, Victoria, Daniel, and Charlotte? We do know, however, what happens to Dantès, and where Emily stands at the end of *Revenge*'s first season.

Despite their differences, the major theme of *The Count of Monte Cristo* and *Revenge* is the same: revenge is not only a stony path, it's a lonely one. Emily and Dantès destroy the lives of their enemies; they reclaim the lives they believe they lost. But when it's all over, they both end up where they began their vengeance plots: with few friends, no family, and money they do not value. Vengeance gives them a mission and a purpose. Without it, Dantès and Emily must look forward and figure out how they can really get back the life they lost.

the revenger

THE PRODIGAL DAUGHTER RETURNS:
EMILY THORNE

When we first meet Emily Thorne, she's a badass hell-bent on avenging her father's name. On a mission that's defined the past decade of her life, she's given up everything — including her identity — in order to accomplish this goal. But Emily is no stone-cold sociopath. She's a girl who is damaged, lost, and searching for meaning.

We meet four versions of Emily Thorne in *Revenge*, and each has her own arc throughout the season: young Amanda Clarke, teenaged Amanda Clarke, adult Amanda Clarke, and Amanda's alter ego, Emily Thorne. Through the eyes of young Amanda, we learn what Emily has lost and why she's so angry. Through teenaged Amanda, we see how Emily comes to understand what happened to her father and how and why she resolves to do something about it. Through adult Amanda Clarke, we watch this plan in action, a plan that plays out via Amanda's alter ego, Emily Thorne.

Emily is driven by her need to avenge her family, perhaps because she hasn't had one since she was nine years old. Young Amanda Clarke's life was idyllic: she had a doting father, a loyal best friend, and an adorable puppy. Over the next 20 years, it became easy — and essential — for her to romanticize those early memories of her life. Young Amanda was a witness to many events she shouldn't have known about, including secret midnight rendezvous and conversations about corruption. Not only do these moments give viewers insight into what was going on with David, Victoria, and Grayson Global before Clarke's arrest, they reinforce the idea that everyone saw Amanda as a harmless, happy child, oblivious to what was going on around her. But we know the truth: Amanda was a keen, quiet, and patient observer even before she had a reason to be, a trait that would aid Amanda later in life.

When Amanda was in her teen years, believing her father was a terrorist responsible for hundreds of deaths, her pleasant childhood memories conflicted with her conception of him. When she learns that her father is innocent of the charges that put him in jail, these memories prove reliable; she must do what she can to protect them. Avenging his honor is not only a way to stay close to him; it's a way to make up for when her faith in his goodness faltered. As our protagonist comes to this decision, we watch her refocus her anger, which was originally directed at her father and at the world for dealing her such a crappy hand, on those who framed her father and stole her happiness and innocence. As a teenager and young adult, Amanda externalizes this anger, beating on her fellow inmates and on people in clubs. But as she begins to focus on her goal of vengeance, this anger is internalized, resulting in Emily's trademark icy stare. She evolves from a volatile, aimless young woman into a woman under control and on a mission.

Her purpose now clear, she resolves not to be distracted or to compromise, and keeps everyone at arm's length. Relationships complicate things. Emily saw what happened to her father with Victoria. But as the season unfolds, it gets harder for Emily to keep her emotions in check and to avoid earnestly engaging in relationships. On the one hand, this opening-up can be seen as going soft. On the other hand, it's Emily's way of reclaiming what she lost so long ago. All her father wanted was for Amanda to be happy. And as Emily realizes that the path to revenge is lonely, she honors her father when she lets others in — just as he did so freely.

These days, those closest to being Emily's family are Nolan Ross and Fauxmanda, two people who love her and want to protect her. But even though Emily holds family in the highest regard, she manipulates and threatens these two. So used to not trusting or relying on anyone, she can't see that Nolan and Fauxmanda are (usually) there for her and (usually) want to help her. Instead, by insisting on doing things her way and forging ahead, Emily drives them away. She believes her my-way-or-the-highway approach protects them and her plan, but often her solo act only makes things more complicated — and dangerous — for all involved.

In a strange way, Emily treats Fauxmanda and Nolan much like Victoria treats her children. Emily loves and cares for them, just as Victoria does for Daniel and Charlotte, but both are quick to use them to get what they want. Emily uses Fauxmanda to get information from Mason Treadwell and uses Nolan to obtain video surveillance of her targets and to encourage Declan to lie on the stand. Victoria uses Daniel to gain an advantage in the divorce proceedings and uses Charlotte to convince Declan to tell the truth during Daniel's trial. And when "the children" act out, Emily and Victoria feel obliged to clean up the mess and repair the relationship they harmed. It's a vicious cycle, but one that gives both women strength, power, and purpose.

Just as Emily idealized and romanticized her father, she does the same to Jack, her childhood best friend. For Emily, Jack represents all that is good in her past. He is the promise she keeps to herself, the hope for contentment after her vengeance has been fulfilled. By protecting him, she safeguards her childhood self too. As Emily's plan gets more and more complicated, keeping Jack from it gets harder and harder to do — he becomes intimately involved, thanks to his feelings (first for her, then for Fauxmanda) and to Emily's own growing affection for him.

The same complications arise with Daniel and Charlotte: Emily believes she can get close to them without caring for them, but she vastly overestimates her sociopathic tendencies. As she plays the part of devoted girlfriend and then fiancée, Daniel comes to represent to her the potential happiness and satisfying relationship she could have if she let go of her anger. He also represents the idea that people can be better than their circumstance: just as Amanda Clarke is more than the daughter of a notorious terrorist, Daniel is more than the heir to the Grayson fortune. Emily grows protective of Charlotte, seeing in her the potential for a real familial relationship, which she's been missing since she was nine years old. Both are lost women, wrestling with having a notorious father and a (differently) absent mother. Charlotte is looking for a connection to David Clarke; if Emily wasn't revenging, she could offer that connection to her and, possibly, find peace herself.

Yet, Emily refuses to soften toward the person she has the most in common with: Victoria. Like Victoria, Emily loved David. Like Victoria, Emily tries to control everyone and everything around her. Like Victoria, Emily does her best to keep her emotions in check. But instead of seeing Victoria as a woman who also lost everything when David Clarke was sent to prison, Emily sees Victoria as having committed the greatest sin of all. She turned her back on David Clarke to protect herself, destroying him in the process. For Emily, a woman defined by her love for and fierce devotion to her father, this is the greatest sin of all.

Which is why Victoria must suffer most of all.

REVENGINATORS
EMILY THORNE'S PREDECESSORS

Emily Thorne is one of the most driven, take-charge characters on the small screen today. But there's a long line of heroes and antiheroes who paved the way for her journey to the Hamptons. Below are the six fictional characters she should thank the most.

Nikita from *Nikita* (1990), *La Femme Nikita* (1997–2001), and *Nikita* (2010–present): The story of Nikita has had several interpretations: the original French film (in which Nikita killed more freely), the cult classic television show (in which Nikita was more innocent) and the modernized CW television remake (which tells Nikita's story after she escapes the secret government organization and seeks revenge on the government agent who stole her life and murdered her fiancé). However, each of these versions of the story has the same core character, a young homeless girl whose suicide is faked by the government and who is then given a choice: she can either become a trained assassin or she can die. In each, she chooses to live. Nikita discovers she has a talent for killing but struggles with the assignments she's given. It's this combination of physical strength, instinct for destruction, and conflicted inner morality that defines the character and her many successors — including Emily Thorne.

Buffy Summers from *Buffy the Vampire Slayer* (1997–2003): Joss Whedon created Buffy Summers, Vampire Slayer, as a response to "the little blonde girl who goes into a dark alley and gets killed in every horror film." He wanted a strong character to shake up the role of women in the action-adventure genre. While he didn't realize his vision with the 1992 movie starring Kristy Swanson, he certainly did with the Sarah Michelle Gellar–led TV show. Buffy destroys the Big Bads, saves the world, and still finds time for messy romantic relationships and hanging out with her friends. Throughout the show's seven seasons, Buffy struggles between accepting her destiny and her own darkness and fighting against it. She's conflicted and complex and, like Emily Thorne, defies everyone's expectations of what a pretty blonde girl can and should be capable of. *Special bonus trivia:* On *Revenge*, the terrorist group responsible for the crash of Flight 197 is called the American Initiative; on *Buffy*, the secret government agency in charge of fighting demons is called the Initiative.

Sydney Bristow from *Alias* (2001–2006): An ass-kicking double agent with daddy *and* mommy issues? Emily Thorne owes a lot to Sydney Bristow, a CIA spy who believed her mother died when she was six. Sydney, like Emily, learns that her mother is indeed alive; on *Alias*, the absentee mom is intimately involved in the organization Sydney is trying to destroy. Sydney spent years training for her role as an agent: she's a master of disguise, multi-lingual, and has a technically adept sidekick. You wouldn't want to mess with Sydney or Emily if you ran into them in a dark alley. *Special bonus trivia:* In the third season, there is an attempt to brainwash Sydney into believing she is an assassin named Julia — you guessed it — Thorne.

Beatrix Kiddo from *Kill Bill: Volume 1* (2003) and *Kill Bill: Volume 2* (2004): Beatrix is better known as "The Bride" from Quentin Tarantino's epic revenge fantasy. Trained as an assassin in a secret team called the Deadly Viper Assassination Squad, Beatrix secretly retires in order to live a regular life with her soon-to-be-born daughter. But on her wedding day, the Squad attacks. Everyone is murdered and Beatrix is left comatose. When she wakes up four years later, she believes her daughter is dead and decides to seek revenge on those who betrayed her, one by one. Tall, blonde, and singly focused on avenging the destruction of their families,

Beatrix and Emily were cut from the same cloth. There's one small difference: Emily wants to destroy her targets' lives. Beatrix wants them all to die.

Veronica Mars from _Veronica Mars_ (2004–2007): Veronica Mars was a teen detective who turned to solving crimes in order to avenge her disgraced father, the former police chief who became a private detective after a botched murder investigation. With its noir feel, whip-smart storytelling, and badass blonde protagonist, _Revenge_ looks and feels like _Veronica Mars: All Grown Up and Madder than Ever_.

Dexter Morgan from _Dexter_ (2006–present): "The best comparison I've had so far was that she's a sort of less homicidal version of Dexter, and that rings so true to me," Emily VanCamp said shortly after _Revenge_ premiered. Why does this comparison work so well? _Dexter_ follows Dexter Morgan, who, unbeknownst to everyone, is a serial killer. The catch? He only kills criminals. Dexter, like Emily Thorne, walks the fine line between avenging angel and sociopath, drawing audiences in with unexpected charisma and a twisted, but understandable, sense of justice. Both use narration to frame each episode, and flashbacks offer insight into the present. Both Dexter and Emily must deal with how their dark choices affect their personal lives, and both are guided by the memories of their fathers. The big difference between the two? Emily Thorne refuses to kill, while Dexter feels most himself with a plastic-wrapped victim in front of him and a knife in hand.

EMILY VANCAMP
AS EMILY THORNE

Emily Irene VanCamp (b. May 12, 1986) is an old soul, at least when it comes to television. *Revenge* is the Port Perry, Ontario, native's third series, after long-running stints on The WB's *Everwood* (2002–2006) and ABC's *Brothers & Sisters* (2007–2010).

Growing up, VanCamp wanted to be a ballerina. At 11 years old, she convinced her parents to let her move to Montreal to study ballet at the prestigious L'École supérieure de ballet du Québec, following in her big sister's toe shoes. In fact, it was following this same big sister to a film set — she had been cast as a background dancer in a local film production — that introduced VanCamp to acting. "It looked so much fun," Emily told *Vanity Fair*. So she signed up for classes, got a manager, and it wasn't long before she was landing local commercials and gave up dance to pursue acting. "I loved it a lot more than dance. So I kind of just went with it."

In 2002, 16-year-old Emily scored her first recurring TV role on the Kevin Williamson show *Glory Days*. The series lasted only nine episodes but VanCamp's performance caught the eye of television writer and producer Greg Berlanti. When Berlanti began developing a new teen drama for The WB, he could imagine only one actress in the part of girl-next-door Amy Abbott: Emily VanCamp. VanCamp spent four years with *Everwood*, a series that told the story of a father and his two kids who moved to fictional Everwood, Colorado, after the devastating loss of their wife and mother. In 2006 when The WB and UPN merged to form The CW, the cast and crew were uncertain of the show's fate — so unsure that they filmed two different endings for the season four finale, just in case. This foresight proved to be the best thing for the show and its fans because when The CW announced their inaugural line-up, *Everwood* wasn't on it. "It was devastating for all of us," VanCamp told the *TV Addict*. But the alternate ending gave fans what they wanted: Amy and her next-door-neighbor Ephram together forever.

After *Everwood*, VanCamp was ready to try something new. She

thought about going back to school or giving a film career a try. But then she got a surprising phone call: Greg Berlanti wanted her to join his latest show, the ABC drama *Brothers & Sisters*, as Rebecca Harper, the illegitimate daughter of the family's patriarch, William Walker. "I really wasn't looking to do television," VanCamp said in 2006. "But . . . I'd have been pretty dumb to pass up an opportunity to work with the likes of Calista Flockhart and Sally Field!" VanCamp enjoyed playing Rebecca as the character offered her new challenges. But after four seasons and with 75 episodes under her belt, VanCamp was done. "I felt my character had run its course," she told the *Hollywood Reporter*, "and it was time to move on." When her contract entered re-negotiation, VanCamp decided not to renew, which she did with the show's and network's blessings. "We love Emily," *Brothers & Sisters* showrunner David Marshall Grant told *Entertainment Weekly* at the time. "She wanted to try other things, and I don't think anyone here wanted to stand in the way of her dreams."

Thanks in part to this amicable departure, VanCamp's name came up as a possible contender for Emily Thorne. For the second time in her career, even though VanCamp wasn't looking to do television, it was a role she knew she couldn't pass up. "I wanted to make sure that the next thing I did was something I was very passionate about. And more importantly, something that challenged me," the actress told *Vanity Fair*. "And when I read *Revenge*, it was all of that and more." This deal wasn't as easy as *Everwood* and *Brothers & Sisters* had been: VanCamp had to fight for the role of Emily Thorne. Her perseverance paid off and VanCamp is relishing the challenge of not only leading the show, but also navigating a complicated character. "It's so much fun," she said. "I get to live vicariously through this character in a weird way, so anyone that I've ever wanted to exact revenge on, I get to just throw it all into the character. It's wonderful."

the targets

Though Emily sets her sights on taking down everyone who betrayed her father, she has two main targets — Conrad and Victoria Grayson — and she won't stop until their lives are destroyed.

THE QUEEN OF THE HAMPTONS:
VICTORIA GRAYSON

When we first meet Victoria, she's a monarch whose rule is in shambles: her marriage is rocky, her relationships with her children strained, her best friend betraying her, and her share of Grayson Global insecure. But, as the season progresses, she moves from desperately hanging on to her power to learning to let go of it, as the foundation of the life she's built is destroyed. When she expels Lydia, she no longer has someone to confide in; when Frank dies, she no longer has someone to protect her; when she divorces Conrad, she no longer has her public persona of the perfect Hamptons matriarch to cultivate; and when both of her children push her away in response to her questionable actions, she has no one to mother. Which each loss, Victoria questions her choices, re-evaluating the cost of her past actions.

Emily's first attack on Victoria is well targeted: Lydia's affair with Conrad shakes Victoria's confidence. Her best friend — someone she should be able to trust and a person who knows her deepest secrets — has betrayed her. It is a stark reminder to Victoria that she can't trust anyone, not even those in her inner circle. Victoria's attack on Lydia, exiling her publicly, reveals to us that even though she appears to be an ice queen, Victoria is rash, passionate, and quick to retaliate. She's just learned how to hide her "weakness," thanks to years of practice. As a result of Lydia's betrayal, Victoria goes on high alert; she doesn't want to be burned again.

The second pillar to collapse under Victoria is Frank, the man who had been by her side for years, doing her dirty work. When Frank is killed, she loses not only her security guard, but someone who knew all her secrets and still put her feelings and safety first. A stand-in for a best friend and husband, Frank's support fueled Victoria's strength and conviction. But with him gone (and possibly murdered as a result of his relationship to the Graysons), Victoria realizes that the person she was closest to was someone she employed. As long as the Graysons are involved in shady activities, the threat of such violence looms, and she begins the tentative first steps toward retribution. After Frank's death, two things happen: Victoria takes matters into her own hands (like hiring Lee Moran to beat up Jack and Daniel) and she is more openly emotional, for better or for worse.

Once a girl "with cheap shoes and limited social graces" herself, Victoria successfully conned her way into a marriage with a powerful and wealthy man. She left a man she loved — the art forger, Dominik Wright — in order to build the life she thought she wanted. Throughout her empty marriage to Conrad, she persevered, believing the status quo was better than any alternative. She held on through her affair with David Clarke. Even when he presented her a second opportunity to choose love, she chooses to stay with Conrad. Victoria wasn't afraid of losing the Grayson riches — let's not forget that David was enormously wealthy too — she was afraid of losing control. When she was with Dominik or with David, she wasn't in control. She was open and loving, which left her vulnerable. But with Conrad sleeping with Lydia and Frank gone, Victoria understands that even with the strongest coat of armor, she still can get hurt. This is why she does what she can to keep the two people that matter most to her in her life: Daniel and Charlotte.

Victoria's need for control dominates her relationships with Daniel and Charlotte. Growing up, Daniel was a dutiful mama's boy. Victoria never had to question her power over him, and Victoria could protect him in the way she thought best without being second-guessed; she swiftly dealt with the messy aftermath of his car accident, ignoring any feelings he may have had for the girl involved. It's only when Emily enters the picture that Victoria begins to lose control over Daniel. And that terrifies Victoria. As she quickly learns, she has no power over Emily: Emily appears invulnerable to her manipulations. To disrupt the blossoming romance, Victoria tells Daniel that Emily just wants the Grayson name, painting her as a money-hungry social climber, but Victoria knows that the opposite is true. Emily doesn't want to be a Grayson. She doesn't need the Grayson name or money or anything that the Graysons have to offer her. And from Victoria's perspective, that makes her incredibly dangerous.

Victoria's appearance as a dutiful wife and mother is a carefully controlled performance. She knows what kind of image she needs to project, and does so; a prime example being her relationship with Charlotte — picture-perfect to outsiders while strained and tense at home. Victoria is the ultimate actress, playing the charming host of extravagant events, the commanding wife to her powerful husband, and the adoring mother of her son and daughter. But Charlotte doesn't want to pretend. She wants a relationship that is authentic, warts and all. Victoria has spent so long hiding her emotions that she struggles with Charlotte's deceptively simple need — especially since Charlotte is the product of one of the more emotional and difficult times in Victoria's life.

As much as Victoria loosens her grip on the people, parties, and things around her as the season progresses, she never gives up control. Instead, she shifts her focus from maintaining her image to exploring her true wants and needs. Kicking her best friend out of the Hamptons, fighting her way through a messy divorce, meddling in her son's relationship and then his trial helped maintain her public image, but those actions do nothing for Victoria's conscience or for the relationships she cares about. And as she sees her children making decisions she disagrees with, she realizes that she can no longer manipulate them. She needs to lead by example — by leaving their father, by telling the truth — and hope her children will make similar decisions.

But old habits die hard, and throughout the season Victoria struggles between who she is and who she wants to be. Take the moment when Victoria tells the truth to Daniel about David Clarke: she's being emotionally honest with him, but when he comes to the wrong conclusion about what happened, she lets it be. If he believes that David Clarke raped her, he'll stand by her side — a lie that Victoria will live with, since it gives her Daniel's devotion again. However, by the time she tells the truth to Charlotte at David's grave, Victoria has turned a corner. She's accepted her past and is willing to share it, completely, with her children. She's realized that's the only chance she has to have them truly stand by her side.

At the core of Victoria's journey over season one is her struggle with her guilt over what she did to David Clarke. As things fall apart, she is reminded that the life she built — the very one that's crumbling around her — exists only because she destroyed someone she loved. As her family distances themselves from her and moves toward those who give them affection, devotion, and support — Conrad to Lydia, Daniel to Emily, and Charlotte to Declan — Victoria realizes her past errors. She gave up that kind of connection when she betrayed David. By the end of the season, she's lost her son, her daughter, and her husband, but she has found a new sense of purpose. Nothing is more important to her than honoring David Clarke and making her past wrongs right.

But is it too little too late?

MADELEINE STOWE
AS VICTORIA GRAYSON

Madeleine Stowe (b. August 18, 1958), like Victoria Grayson, goes after what she wants. Born Madeline M. Stowe in a suburb of Los Angeles to an Oregonian father and a Costa Rican mother (who can claim a Costa Rican president in her lineage), Stowe never dreamed of being an actress. Growing up, she wanted to be a concert pianist. But when her instructor died when Stowe was 18 years old, she couldn't continue and threw herself into other pursuits. "I just felt it was time to not be by myself anymore," she told *Entertainment Weekly*. Always intrigued by storytelling, Stowe enrolled in the film and journalism program at the University of Southern California. School proved to be less than satisfying, and she turned to another storytelling outlet: community theater. It was there, handing out playbills, that she was discovered by an agent. Stowe made her television debut shortly thereafter in a 1978 episode of *Baretta*. Plenty of TV guest roles followed, including *The Amazing Spider-Man* (1978), *Barnaby Jones* (1979), and *Little House on the Prairie* (1980). The frequent work helped her personal life as much as her professional one. During the filming of the 1981 TV movie *The Gangster Chronicles*, she met her future husband, *Private Practice* star Brian Benben.

After a decade in television, Stowe made the jump to films. Thanks to a head-turning starring role in the 1987's *Stakeout* opposite Richard Dreyfuss, Stowe became a member of Hollywood's elite. For the next 10 years, she worked with A-list stars like Kevin Costner in *Revenge* (1990), Jack Nicholson in *The Two Jakes* (1990), Kurt Russell in *Unlawful Entry* (1992), Daniel Day-Lewis in *The Last of the Mohicans* (1992), and Brad Pitt and Bruce Willis in *12 Monkeys* (1995). Stowe's career had never been better. But after the birth of her daughter, May, in 1996, she decided to switch her focus from her career to her family life. "I had never considered leaving the business," she said to the *Los Angeles Times*. "But after I had May, something just sort of broke in me a little bit." She became more selective about the projects she worked on and eventually moved to a ranch in rural Texas. "There were other things I wanted to do, other lives I wanted to live," Stowe explained to *More* magazine. "I just got to the point where I wanted to be somewhere else."

Her family spent several happy, low-key years in Texas before returning to Los Angeles. While living in Texas, Stowe penned her *piece d'resistance*, a western thriller called *The Unbound Captives*. She originally intended

to star in the project, but decided to focus on directing and producing it. Rachel Weisz signed on to play the role Stowe had written for herself, and *The Unbound Captives* is expected to hit theaters in 2013 or 2014. Stowe had seen how horrible Hollywood was for women of a certain age and didn't want to participate as an actress. She was ready for the next phase of her career. "I had given up the idea of wanting to be an actress," she said. But her agent wasn't so sure. He thought Stowe could find the kind of dynamic and interesting character she was looking for in television. He asked her to look at pilot scripts for the fall 2011 season and, after much convincing, she agreed. Only one spoke to her, a Mike Kelley–penned, under-the-radar project called *Revenge*. "I thought the character was very twisted and compelling. She's not like anyone I've ever seen before," Stowe said to the *Los Angeles Times*. She gave Kelley and the producers a call. They jumped at the chance to cast her, and one of the most memorable characters to grace the small screen in recent memory was born. Despite her initial reservation against a full-time commitment after so many years of working sporadically, Stowe couldn't be happier to be back on TV. "These characters intrigue me. It's just a fun, gripping ride."

THE BAD GUY BOSS:
CONRAD GRAYSON

When asked about Conrad Grayson's motives, Henry Czerny told the *TV Fanatic*, "As long as the game is interesting to Conrad, he's in it. And if he has to defend what he's earned, he will play it to the death." Conrad needs to win.

This desire to win is what propels him to work so hard, growing his father's company into a global corporation. It's why he built the biggest house in the Hamptons, remains married to a woman he no longer loves, and encourages his children to project images of happiness and success. It all helps Conrad feel he is winning in the game of life. But it also leads him to engage in shady business practices and hop into bed with Lydia.

If you screw with Conrad (as Victoria has time and time again), Conrad will screw you (or your best friend) right back.

Throughout the first season of *Revenge*, we watch the life Conrad built crumble around him: his marriage falls apart, his relationship with his daughter falls apart, and then his company falls apart. Though he tries to repair what's damaged, the more messed-up things become, the more he looks for alternatives to replace what he has lost: he reunites with Lydia, he focuses on his son, and he looks to get out of town to protect himself from the Grayson Global fall-out. Conrad is a survivor. Knock him down and he'll get right back up again, looking for new ways into the game and more determined than ever to win.

Although Conrad's relationship with Victoria completely deteriorates by the end of the season, it's clear he once loved her. "I really never have loved any woman the way I've loved you," he tells her. He left his first wife for her. He destroyed a man for her. He gave her everything she ever wanted. But when Victoria couldn't give Conrad the only thing he asked for — to be loved back and for them to be on the same team — he looked elsewhere: by having a discreet affair with Lydia, then agreeing to a divorce. As Victoria becomes less willing to contribute to the façade of a happy family, Conrad becomes more determined to freeze her out.

He's a man who prides himself on his public image, and his children are a part of that. If they succeed, it means Conrad is succeeding, as a father and as a provider. This is why he struggles so much with the news that Charlotte is not his biologically: daddy's little girl turns out to be David Clarke's love child. He could count on his relationship with Charlotte: she fiercely loves her father and would turn to him in time of need. But Charlotte becomes a living, breathing reminder of Victoria's betrayal and that the picture-perfect empire he has built is a house of cards that could crash at any moment. After he first pushes Charlotte away, his sense of familial duty prevails — a family is more than the DNA you share — and he offers Charlotte what she's looking for: an unwavering sense of commitment, protection, and affection. But until Charlotte figures out her own identity issues, she won't be able to accept that there's a difference between the father who created you and the father who raised you.

While Charlotte was always a "daddy's girl," Conrad's relationship with Daniel was initially more strained. When Daniel returns from school, the father-son dynamic is tense as Conrad tries to shape Daniel's future and his son rejects his control. It turns combative when Daniel sides with Victoria in the divorce. But, by the end of the season, Daniel is, wholly and truly, Conrad's son, a complicit participant in the Grayson secrets and a dutiful employee of Grayson Global. After struggling under the yoke of "what it means to be a Grayson," Daniel gives his father commitment and respect — what Conrad never felt he had from his father or from Victoria. Instead he felt they had contempt for him, believing he wasn't able to provide for his family or run his company. But Daniel sees his father's worst and chooses to follow him like he's a true leader. Though Charlotte adores Conrad, a young girl's love for her father is not as meaningful to Conrad as Daniel's conscious choice to stand by his side, no matter what. Will Daniel's newfound loyalty to the good ship Grayson be enough to save it from sinking?

HENRY CZERNY
AS CONRAD GRAYSON

Henry Czerny (b. February 8, 1959) likes playing the bad guy. "I might be an imbecile," he said to the *New York Times*, "but I've never refused a role because the character is a bad guy. I've refused roles because they're too simplistic." It's a strategy that's worked well for the renowned actor, who has two Geminis (the Canadian version of the Emmys) on his mantle. Before relocating to Los Angeles, the Toronto, Ontario, native made a name for himself in his home country performing in the Stratford Shakespeare Festival and in Canadian productions like the acclaimed TV movie *The Boys of St. Vincent* (1992).

It was his turn in *The Boys of St. Vincent* that booked him a ticket to Hollywood. An agency on the hunt for undervalued talent noticed his performance as a priest who molests a young boy and put him in front of director Phillip Noyce, who was casting for his 1994 film, *Clear and*

42   best served cold

Present Danger. Czerny made an impression, got the part, and his career changed forever. Since then, he's worked consistently in both Canadian and American productions like *The Ice Storm* (1997), *The Pink Panther* (2006), and *The A-Team* (2010), but is best known to movie-goers as villain Eugene Kittridge, the man who utters the infamous line "your mission, should you choose to accept it . . ." in *Mission: Impossible* (1996).

Throughout his 25-year career, Czerny had made the occasional guest appearance on television, including a 10-episode run as the Duke of Norfolk on *The Tudors* in 2007, but *Revenge* is his first full-time small-screen gig. "[TV] requires a very different set of muscles," he said to Washington radio show *The Key*. "You need to dance a lot quicker and with a lot more finesse."

the collateral damage

Before Emily moved to the Hamptons, she saw the Grayson heirs as nothing more than rich, spoiled brats who deserved destruction as much as their parents did. After all, Daniel and Charlotte directly (though unwittingly) benefited from their parents' criminal activities: a gorgeous summer home, a world-class education, and fancy clothes and cars. But as Emily gets to know the Grayson kids, they are no longer abstractions. They are real people full of complexity. She soon sees that they too have been hurt by Conrad and Victoria — just in different ways — and that makes vengeance that much more difficult.

THE PRINCELY PUPPET:
DANIEL GRAYSON

When Daniel tells Emily, "No one said I can't be my own man and my father's son," he believes it. But as Daniel struggles to understand what it means to be both his "own man" and his "father's son" throughout *Revenge*'s first season, he realizes it's not so easy to separate the two.

Daniel's journey has three acts: first, he's the reformed bad boy eager to prove he's changed, then he's the murder suspect eager to prove he's innocent, and finally he's indeed a Grayson, eager to prove he's worthy of a place at the boardroom table. But as Daniel struggles to prove himself and establish his identity, he's undermined by the fact that he's getting played, constantly, by those who are supposed to love and support him.

He spends much of the summer trying on different hats and seeing if they fit. Is he a poet? A bartender? A shrewd businessman? A big reason why Daniel dates — and falls for — Emily is because she isn't interested in him because he's a Grayson, but because he's *Daniel*. She's unfamiliar with his reputation and has a pedigree that rivals his own. (Or so she quite wily leads him to believe.)

Daniel is so eager to believe that Emily is everything he wants, because he wants to see the best in people. Daniel expects loyalty and honesty from his mother, his fiancée, his best friend, and his father. However, Daniel's tendency to give people the benefit of the doubt proves to be misguided again and again. In fact, it has the worst possible outcome for him: he's charged with murder.

It's during the murder investigation that Daniel's worldview finally shatters. Not only is he grappling with Tyler's betrayal and Emily's secrets, he comes to understand that the world sees him as a privileged young man and is really angry about it. People who don't even know him think they have his number. If complete strangers want him to suffer, defining him by his wealth and last name, why should he try to be any-more than that? After all, his wealth and last name *are* what makes him and his life special — the feeling he was looking for when he was quoting poetry in the college bar and when he was begging Emily to run away to Paris with him.

Daniel ends up embracing his place in the boardroom because that choice provides a solution to what he's struggled with all season. When Conrad lays the truth out for his son, he is giving Daniel the opportunity to *choose* to be a Grayson, eyes open. It never was the "Grayson" part of the equation that bothered Daniel: it was the lack of choice in the matter. By electing to be a Grayson, Daniel can tell himself that he's more than his last name: he's loyal, he's dedicated, and he's willing to do what it takes to stand by his family.

As Daniel finds himself doubtful of and disappointed in those he once trusted blindly, he gravitates to the one person who is always honest with him: his father. All season long, the people he trusted the most — his fiancée, his best friend, and his mother — lied to him, cheated on him, and played him. Daniel is taken advantage of over and over again. When confronted by Daniel, Conrad does something Tyler, Emily, or Victoria never did: he tells him the truth. Daniel can accept Conrad's criminal acts, because of his motivation: he did it all to protect his family. He was loyal to the Grayson name. By spilling the Grayson secrets, Conrad puts a confidence in his son that is strong enough for Daniel to completely reject his mother, choose the course of action that distances him from Emily, and embrace his name and the legacy that comes with it.

Protecting the family name gives Daniel the purpose he's spent all summer seeking. By the end of the season, he's become wise to the fact that people aren't always who they pretend to be. Now, if he can use his money, status, and power to his advantage — as he tries to do with Jack Porter — he will, which is something Daniel would have never done before his trial. He's in the game and willing to use whatever he has at his disposal to win. What Daniel has yet to realize is that the Graysons are simply pawns in someone else's game.

 ## JOSH BOWMAN
AS DANIEL GRAYSON

Joshua Tobias Bowman (b. March 4, 1988) may play all-American royalty on *Revenge*, but in real life, his allegiance lies with the queen of England. The Berkshire, U.K., born and bred actor grew up dreaming of a rugby career. It's a dream that came true, for a while. He played professionally until several injuries sidelined him at the age of 19. When facing a rugby-free future, an agent friend encouraged Bowman to try acting, and he hasn't looked back. "I loved the performing arts in high

school but had no experience besides that," he told *GQ*. "I guess the universe was telling me something." Bowman made his debut in the 2007 Nickelodeon UK series *Genie in the House* before spending two years on the BBC series *Holby City* (2009–2010). A few more small parts on film and TV followed before he decided to head to New York to try to make it in America. He landed a recurring role as bisexual gymnast Max on the second season of ABC Family's *Make It or Break It* (2011) before swapping the gym for the beach to play Daniel Grayson on *Revenge*.

"What you see is what you get" with Daniel, Bowman said, and, as an actor, he's eager to see his character branch out. But he's enjoying his newfound fame and the challenge of adding layers and nuance to what could be a one-dimensional character. "I'm trying to make him more interesting," he told *Assignment X* as the first season debuted. "I want people to want to watch me on TV. I want people to take an interest and invest in my character."

THE POOR LITTLE RICH GIRL:
CHARLOTTE GRAYSON

"I'm sick of the same. I want different." When Charlotte Grayson says this to Declan Porter at the beginning of the summer, she's being glib. What she didn't realize was just how different her life was about to get.

When we meet Charlotte, she's the stereotypical rich kid. She has everything — an adoring boyfriend, a world-class education, a killer wardrobe, a stunning beach house, and a $200,000 car — and wants the one thing she doesn't have: her parents' love and attention. Despite this gaping hole, Charlotte has a firm understanding of who she is, what she wants, and what she can get away with. This is why she's originally attracted to Declan. He offers her the "different" she's looking for. He's an easy way to rebel against her high society life. He's unpolished and unpretentious — and guaranteed to upset her parents. Charlotte is rebellious, but she doesn't yet cross the line into true bad-girl behavior. She wants to grab her parents' attention, to step out from behind Daniel's shadow, without straying too far from their good graces.

All that changes when Charlotte makes two major discoveries: that Victoria (at least occasionally) regrets having her and that David Clarke is her biological father. Her life is no longer about being a Grayson and taking advantage of that privilege; it's about dealing with who she is and where she might belong. Declan becomes a lifeline for Charlotte: he's the one person who sees her for who she truly is, loves her no matter what, and isn't connected to what happened with David Clarke. But as Charlotte's world spins out of control, Declan's love and support isn't enough and Charlotte turns to other, increasingly desperate, measures to deal with what she's going through. She almost gets arrested, she moves in with her father, she tries to move in with her boyfriend, she becomes obsessed with David Clarke, she uses sex for leverage, and she turns to pills.

Pills are the big attention-getter: her parents worry about her, her grandfather pays attention to her, and family therapy sessions are on the agenda. Pills are the ultimate way to reclaim control, allowing her to manage her feelings. When Charlotte is high, her rejection and loneliness are numbed. Her addiction is also a way to feel connected to her mother and both her fathers. "I guess we can add 'teen pill popper' to the Grayson book of shame," she says to Victoria, but she's only half-joking. As Charlotte watches everyone around her crumble, she begins to believe she ought to crumble too. She has the Grayson name and Clarke DNA: shouldn't she be miserable?

After all, every other Grayson is miserable, especially the one Charlotte spent all season rebelling against: Victoria. Mother and daughter share more than blood: Victoria is Charlotte's closest connection to David Clarke, and Victoria's to David. Charlotte reminds Victoria of her affair with David, her betrayal of Conrad, and her betrayal of David. Victoria's distance from her daughter, questioning her birth to her psychiatrist and being cool to her, stems from that secret. But once the truth is out, their tie to David Clarke is what brings them together.

In many ways, Charlotte represents a young Victoria. Charlotte has

the opportunity to either avoid or make the mistakes Victoria made. While Victoria chose a certain lifestyle over love when she left Dominik for Conrad, Charlotte chooses love over her lifestyle when she leaves Adam for Declan. Charlotte doesn't want to end up like her mother, but by forging her own path, she's reinforcing just how alike she and her mother are. Both want what they don't have and both will do whatever it takes to get it. And when Declan leaves her, Charlotte, like her mother, realizes she can't rely on anyone else to make her happy. The only person she can rely on is herself.

As Charlotte faces disappointment and hardship, she becomes even more like Victoria. She recognizes the power and freedom in punishing and manipulating others. Victoria long ago learned that if she can't be happy, she might as well be in control. By taking down Declan's new friend Jaime, Charlotte feels the surge of victory and twinge of remorse her mother has long grown accustomed to.

At summer's end, Charlotte's world is upside down: she's alone, angry, and scared. And she's dealing with it in the same way Victoria once would have: eagerly hurting others, but hurting herself most of all.

CHRISTA B. ALLEN
AS CHARLOTTE GRAYSON

Christa Brittany Allen (b. November 11, 1991) wanted to act for as long as she can remember. And she gave up a lot to make her dreams come true — instead of field trips, she went on auditions; instead of prom, she spent her time on film sets. It's a sacrifice she's happy she made. "This is what I love to do," she said to *StarPulse*. "I'm fortunate enough to be doing it now at this age." The youngest of nine (Allen has four older brothers and four older step-brothers), she got her start doing commercials and TV guest spots. Her big break came when, at 12 years old, she was cast as a younger Jennifer Garner in *13 Going on 30* (2004). Rounding out her résumé are a handful of film and television roles, including *Grey's Anatomy* (2008), *Wizards of Waverly Place* (2009), *Ghosts of Girlfriends*

Past (2009) — again playing a younger Garner — and *Cold Case* (2010). It wasn't until she landed the role of Charlotte Grayson, however, that people began noticing Allen for her acting skills and not for her startling resemblance to the *Alias* star.

When Allen read the *Revenge* script, she was impressed with the writing and intrigued by Charlotte's potential as a character. "I saw in Charlotte a chance to have a lot of fun with a character. So I was in," she told the *TV Chick*. Like many of her cast mates, *Revenge* is Allen's first major television role, and she's enjoying the new adventure and the attachment fans have to the show and her character. "When people begin to identify with what Charlotte's going through, it makes me feel like our work is not in vain," she said to the *TV Addict*. "We're connecting with people."

the allies

Emily Thorne may act like she's a lone wolf, but she'd be lost in the woods without a little help from her friends: her ever-loyal sidekick, tech maven and billionaire Nolan Ross, and her all-knowing and mysterious mentor, Satoshi Takeda.

THE SIDEKICK:
NOLAN ROSS

With his nouveau-riche status, super modern beach house, and Justin Bieber bangs, Nolan Ross stands out in the Hamptons. But all he really wants is to fit in.

Over the course of the season, Nolan becomes increasingly comfortable with his outsider status, thanks to his growing relationship with Emily and the Porter brothers. His desire to fit in was never about social status: he wanted to feel like he belonged somewhere and he finally does with Emily, Declan, and Jack. By watching Emily take down the

Graysons, he learns that being at the top isn't all it's cracked up to be — and being on the outside can sometimes make you the ultimate insider.

When we first meet Nolan, his dedication to honoring David Clarke and looking out for Emily is bizarre, but we eventually learn why he's so motivated. His family rejected him after he dropped out of college to follow his dreams. Investor after investor turned him down. Then David Clarke came along. Nolan is fiercely loyal to those who stood by him as he built his company from the ground up — his aunt Carole and David Clarke.

Nolan is loyal, but he's also lonely. Without family or real friends, thanks partly to his social awkwardness and partly to the fact that when people look at Nolan "all they see is dollar signs" (as Emily points out to Bill Harmon), he craves companionship and is willing to pay. Nolan is fine with people wanting his money (see: his relationship with Tyler) and he's comfortable with buying friendship (see: his first forays with Jack), but he wants the transactions to be upfront and straightforward. He's all too aware that everyone in the Hamptons has an agenda, and he plays on his own terms.

This means his relationships are a little strange. Nolan develops loyalty to Jack for two reasons. First, Jack isn't impressed with his money, status, or power. He thinks Nolan is a vapid, self-centered one percenter and he lets Nolan know this. For a man who is used to having his ass either kissed or ignored, Jack's candor is refreshing. Nolan wants a friend, someone who will be straight with him and call him on his crap. As strange and one-sided as that makes their relationship in the beginning, Jack and Nolan become true friends. Second, Nolan's money displaced the Porters, and he wants to make sure they don't suffer further because of his ignorance and greed. Nolan is eager to atone for what he did: he knows money won't change Jack's attitude toward him, but it's a small way to pay back the Porters for taking their home a decade earlier.

Nolan's only other friendship is the strangest one of all. Emily Thorne's not particularly pleasant or forthcoming with him. But standing by Emily (whether she likes it or not) is Nolan's way of paying back David Clarke for the faith he showed in Nolan's vision 20 years ago. A relationship formed by their shared loyalty to Emily's father and a desire to clear his name, Nolan and Emily's friendship eventually grows, based on a shared understanding and like-minded goals — it just takes a while to get to mutual respect.

Like Emily, Nolan wants to see those who did wrong suffer: David, the one person who believed in him, died in prison reviled and hated, and his beloved aunt Carole was forced to fake her death and spend decades in hiding. But he also enjoys the voyeuristic nature of his role as Emily's sidekick. The desire for revenge is a universal feeling. We've all experienced it, but few of us have acted on it. In this way, Nolan is a stand-in for the *Revenge* audience. He has intimate access to Emily's plans, he gets to comment on and question every detail. He gets to live out his revenge fantasies without lighting a match or wielding an ax, because he has his own little sociopath to do it for him.

Don't we all wish we had one of those?

A BILLIONAIRE'S BACKSTORY
NOLAN ROSS

Several self-made billionaires have been cited as inspirations for Nolan Ross. While the character was initially envisioned as a clean-cut college dropout, Nolan evolved into a more eccentric and devious character à la Howard Hughes during *Revenge*'s early stages. Below, find a few sources of inspiration the *Revenge* crew and Gabriel Mann draw from to flesh out the character. But remember: Nolan Ross is unlike anyone we've ever seen before. And he likes it that way.

Mark Zuckerberg: Facebook inventor Mark Zuckerberg (b. May 14, 1984) just might be North America's best-known self-made billionaire. He launched Facebook from his Harvard dorm room in 2004, and it's now the most popular social networking site in existence. Zuckerberg is

also considered one of the most influential people in the world; he was named *Time*'s Person of the Year in 2010. His reputation is almost as famous as the site he built, and he's renowned for his overly casual sartorial style (Nolan Ross would not approve), cagey public attitude, and controlling approach to the Facebook brand and company.

Steve Jobs: If Nolan Ross's uniform is a double-popped collar and matching pocket square, Steve Jobs' uniform was a black turtleneck and jeans. Jobs (b. February 24, 1955) was inseparable from the company he founded, Apple. He changed how people used and thought about technology. Despite his early struggles with Apple (which caused him to leave in 1985 and return in 1996), Jobs oversaw the development of the iMac, iTunes, iPod, iPhone, and iPad. Nolan could learn a lot from the enigmatic, mysterious, and notoriously private Jobs about how to embrace his legacy, lead his company, and continue to push creative and technological boundaries.

Howard Hughes: Howard Hughes (b. December 24, 1905) was, at one point, one of the wealthiest men in the world. Known for his wildly eccentric and reclusive behavior (thanks, in part, to his struggle with OCD and chronic pain), Hughes dabbled in many activities, including film production, charity work, aviation, and investing. As a film producer, he made controversial but industry-defining movies like *Hell's Angels* (1930), *Scarface* (1932), and *The Outlaw* (1943). As a pilot, he set several world records for airspeed and built top-of-the-line aircrafts. He was a visionary, an outcast, ahead of his time, and an impeccable dresser — the Nolan Ross of his era.

Larry Page and Sergey Brin: The Google inventors met while studying for their Ph.D.s in computer science at Stanford University in 1995. When a research project — building the ultimate search engine — began taking over their dorm room and lives, they put their studies on hold to start a company and set up Google out of a friend's garage. While Page (b. March 26, 1973) and Brin (b. August 21, 1973) don't have a mythology comparable to Zuckerberg, Jobs, Hughes, or the fictional Ross, they did lend Nolan one essential biographical element: David Clarke's initial investment in NolCorp is similar to the $100,000 Andy Bechtolsheim invested in Page and Brin's company in 1998 — before Google Inc. was even founded. Page and Brin were just no-name Ph.D. dropouts with big dreams like Ross was when David Clarke invested in his idea. And, like Ross, Page and Brin went on to become leaders in their field who changed the face of their industry.

GABRIEL MANN AS NOLAN ROSS

It may be hard to believe, but the man who plays awkward but lovable Nolan Ross got his start as a fashion model. After years of posing for the camera, Gabriel Mann (b. May 14, 1972) made the transition to acting in front of it in 1995 when he was cast in the film *Parallel Sons*. The Vermont native kept busy with film roles such as Owen in *Great Expectations* (1998), Alan M. in *Josie and the Pussycats* (2001), and Zorn in *The Bourne Identity* (2002) and *The Bourne Supremacy* (2004). While Mann's focus was on films, he also guest-starred on notable television series including *ER* (1997), *Fantasy Island* (1999), and *Carnivale* (2003). Before hitting the Hamptons, he had most recently completed a four-episode stint as Arthur Case on *Mad Men* (2010).

Before *Revenge* came along, Mann was growing frustrated with his career. He felt he was being typecast and was ready to give up on acting all together. But, like many others, he saw the recent creative resurgence on television. "I noticed I had been watching a lot more TV and that a lot of the people I worked with in films were now in television," he told the *TV Chick*. He decided to see if any regular roles up for grabs in the fall 2011 pilot season would interest him before giving up acting altogether. "It was like, well why don't you read some scripts this year and see if you respond to anything." His agent sent him four scripts. Mann, a fan of Mike Kelley and *Swingtown*, was immediately intrigued by Nolan and *Revenge*.

Considered by many to be the show's breakout star, Mann is thrilled at the chance to play a character that audiences around the world have responded to. "Nolan is a character that has been so fun to play that I'm really proud of and so different from me and anything I had really done before," he said to *E! Online*. "It makes it really special."

THE SENSEI:
SATOSHI TAKEDA

Emily may seem ice cold but, compared to her revenge mentor, her blood is boiling. Takeda believes Emily will succeed only if she keeps to her path, completely eliminating any emotional attachment to her targets and those around them. He represents extreme dedication to one's mission and shows us just how much farther Emily needs to go to be a truly dedicated revenge-seeker.

Takeda believes Emily has two problems: Daniel and Jack. For Takeda, they are, at the least, distractions that must be ignored and, at the most, obstacles that should be eliminated. Takeda knows all too well that if Emily's plan works, she won't be settling down for a happy little life with Jack or maintaining any sort of relationship with Daniel. She will have told too many lies and destroyed too many lives for that to happen. Emily strays from Takeda's path, believing she can seek revenge and indulge her emotions, destroy lives and protect them. Takeda disagrees, and by releasing pregnant Fauxmanda back into the Hamptons at the end of the season, he gives Emily one last reminder that she can't have it both ways. She has to make a choice.

Takeda, the stone-cold killer, also represents Emily's possible future. He's in the Hamptons on a moment's notice, putting Emily's plan ahead of whatever mysterious personal relationships or responsibilities he may have in Japan. He kills someone he hardly knows and hides away a relatively innocent girl simply because they know too much. He puts accomplishing one's mission above forgiveness, compassion, or clemency.

As Emily stands before the rabbit hole that is the American Initiative conspiracy, she has two options: to end this quest and start a new life or to jump in. The deeper she falls, the more Takeda-like she'll have to be if she ever wants to emerge again.

SENSEI-TIONAL INFLUENCES
SATOSHI TAKEDA'S PREDECESSORS

To be a good fighter, you need a good teacher. Satoshi Takeda is just the latest in a long line of wise, other-worldly, and morally questionable mentors in popular culture. While Takeda was included to make *Revenge* more appealing to Japanese audiences, he also adds depth and mystery to Emily's backstory. "We wanted her to essentially learn the art of revenge at the foot of somebody who spent years studying it," producer Marty Bowen said. "It sets the tone for the audience to realize, 'Wow, Emily's been to a lot of places before she's gotten here.'" Below are five senseis Emily — and Takeda — should bow down to.

Ra's al Ghul from Batman (1971–present): Ra's al Ghul is a criminal mastermind and Batman's advisor-turned-enemy. Like Takeda, he is extremely wealthy. He is an excellent fighter in many disciplines and is the leader of an organized group of assassins (known in some incarnations as the League of Shadows). This is the group Bruce Wayne turns to in order to understand the criminal mind. Ra's al Ghul trains Wayne in the ways of the League. When Wayne begins to question al Ghul's philosophies and methods, he returns home to Gotham City and becomes Batman, where he eventually learns that al Ghul is planning to destroy the city he calls home. Even though the two are now sworn enemies, al Ghul sees Batman as a potential successor. This love/hate relationship between al Ghul and Batman parallels Takeda and Emily's own relationship — and sets up a scary precedent for what may lie ahead for Emily.

Yoda from Star Wars (1977–2005): Yoda is the mysterious Jedi master who trains Jedi knights, including Luke Skywalker and Anakin Skywalker, and who sits on the Jedi council. Yoda shares many characteristics with Satoshi Takeda, including a mastery of their field, a clipped and unusual manner of speaking, a penchant for pearls of wisdom, and a strong belief that their students must exhibit patience, commitment, and absolute presence of mind in order to succeed.

Splinter from Teenage Mutant Ninja Turtles (1984–present): Splinter is the wise and patient mentor of Donatello, Leonardo, Raphael, and Michelangelo, a team of crime-fighting turtles. Oh, and he's a rat who used to be the pet of — or actually used to *be*, it depends on the origin story — ninja Hamato Yoshi. Splinter can be scarily calm, even when he is angry. He treats the Ninja Turtles like his own children, and he goes out of his way to protect them. Splinter's loyalty to his students is mimicked in Takeda's to Emily. While it's unclear whether Takeda likes or even respects Emily, it's evident he is loyal to her. He does everything he can to fix her mistakes, even when her actions have disappointed him — and even when she doesn't want his help. Splinter wouldn't expect anything less.

Mr. Miyagi from the Karate Kid (1984, 1986, 1989, and 1994): Keisuke Miyagi is a karate master who immigrated to the United States from Japan. He dispenses his philosophical wisdom and martial arts knowledge to his students, Daniel LaRusso (in *The Karate Kid* and its two sequels) and Julie Pierce (in *The Next Karate Kid*). Initially a reluctant teacher, Mr. Miyagi eventually becomes a father figure to his students. It's his combination of dedication, physical strength, and philosophical wisdom that makes him such an effective mentor, and this style is similar to Satoshi Takeda's (much more ominous) method of teaching.

Pai Mei from *Kill Bill: Volume 1* (2003) and *Kill Bill: Volume 2* (2004): An expert in the martial art of Bak Mei, Pai Mei trained many members of the Deadly Viper Assassination Squad, including Beatrix, Bill, and Elle Driver. Pai Mei is an excellent and thorough teacher, but hates pretty much everyone. Like Takeda with Emily, Pai Mei keeps many secrets from his students, and it is difficult for them to earn his trust or his belief in their abilities. While initially a reluctant teacher of Beatrix, Pai Mei eventually comes around, and she becomes his most successful student — which bodes well for Emily's relationship with Takeda.

HIROYUKI SANADA
AS SATOSHI TAKEDA

Like his *Revenge* character, Hiroyuki Sanada (b. October 12, 1960) lives a double life. He's an action star in his home country — Mike Kelley calls him "the Harrison Ford of Japan" — and in North America, he's a respected character actor. And, like his *Revenge* character, when Sanada puts his mind to something, it gets done. When he was 11 years old, he decided to become an action star and began training in martial arts for that very purpose. His hard work paid off. He's best known in Japan for *Kaitō Ruby* (1988), *Ring* (1998) — which was remade in the United States as *The Ring* in 2002 — and *Tasogare Seibei* (2002). After nearly two decades of success in action movies, Sanada decided to branch out. He spent a year in Britain where he played the Fool in the Royal Shakespeare Company's production of *King Lear*, earning an honorary Order of the British Empire. After perfecting his English in the U.K., Sanada headed to Hollywood. His American film credits include *The Last Samurai* (2003) with Tom Cruise, *Rush Hour 3* (2007) with pal Jackie Chan, and *Speed Racer* (2008). However, he's best known to American audiences for his role as Dogen, an influential Other, from the final season of ABC's *Lost* (2010).

the innocent

When Emily first arrives in the Hamptons, she isn't expecting her childhood bestie and his family to still be around. This surprise throws a big curveball in her plans: not only does she try her best not to hurt them, their presence makes Emily step back and take stock of what she's doing.

THE CHILDHOOD SWEETHEART:
JACK PORTER

The Porters are the antithesis of the Graysons. While the Graysons represent all that went wrong in Emily's life — and all that is wrong in the world — Jack represents the good. He's dedicated to his family and friends, he tries to set an example for his brother, and he goes out of his way to be nice to the new girl in town, even when she isn't so welcoming in return.

In the first season, Jack moves from desperately hanging on to the past to looking forward to the future. He's not a fan of change — he puts off his Haiti trip repeatedly and he's not keen to sell the Stowaway — but he has his reasons for that. (But at least he changed his hair. That 2002 cut was terrible!)

First, he wants to make sure his decisions are the right ones for him and for Declan. Second, he doesn't think his life or Montauk is all that bad. Third, he's hoping that Amanda Clarke will come back one day, just as she promised.

Which shows all too well that Jack doesn't know how to let go. He's still longing for a girl he last saw when she was nine. He's hanging onto a floundering bar to honor his father's memory. While his loyalty to his family is admirable, it prevents him from growing. Scared of what he doesn't yet know or understand, Jack could end up realizing Declan's biggest fear: he could turn into their father.

But when Amanda returns (well, it's really Fauxmanda, but Jack doesn't know that), it's everything Jack ever wanted and gives meaning to his lifelong dedication to her. Fauxmanda's presence encourages him to loosen up, and Jack tries to live in the moment. He goes from being cautious and responsible, taking care of his father, his brother, and the bar, to a man driven by his emotions and making reckless decisions. Enraptured by the idea of Amanda, he overlooks their problems; when he feels like he's losing her, he throws rhyme and reason out the window in a desperate attempt to get answers. He storms into a Grayson dinner party and tells off the Queen of the Hamptons. He incriminates himself in a legal investigation and even keeps the evidence that ties him to a crime scene. He chases Fauxmanda all over the country. For so long, Jack had kept everything bottled up inside, but through his relationship with Fauxmanda, he's realized that doing that means missing out on living his life. That's partly why Jack's so desperate to get her back. When Fauxmanda is around, he abandons a lot of his responsibilities. If she's really the one, then it should all be worth it, right?

Once he accepts that she might be gone for good and realizes his obsession with Amanda meant he was neglecting other, more important matters, Jack resets his priorities. Declan is still a kid and needs a father figure, someone who can give him a future worth looking forward to. He comes to understand that there's a disconnect between the ideal Amanda he had dreamed of and the reality of Fauxmanda. With Fauxmanda gone, he can finally let go and sail to Haiti — or pursue that other girl he's had his eye on, Emily.

With his heart on his sleeve and an eye to the future like never before,

Jack is open to possibility. This is why he completely breaks down over Sammy's death. It's not only the death of his oldest best friend, but symbolic of everything else Jack is saying good-bye to: his overburdened sense of responsibility, his closed-off nature, his possibility of a future with Amanda. That emotional release allows for connection with Emily; the good-hearted honorable Jack from early in season one would never have made out with an engaged woman. Jack realizes that by being the polite guy waiting in the wings, he's always going to get passed over. Emily chose Daniel and Fauxmanda chose to disappear. But if Jack goes after what he wants, maybe he will find the happiness he deserves.

However, that goes out the window when Fauxmanda arrives back in town, with her pregnant belly. It looks like Jack might not escape the weight of responsibility after all. But maybe he doesn't want to. After all, being the good guy everyone can rely on is who he's always been. And if we've learned anything over the course of the first season, it's that Jack's not so good with change.

NICK WECHSLER
AS JACK PORTER

Fans of *Roswell* (1999–2002) squealed with delight when they saw that Nick Wechsler (b. September 3, 1978) was back on TV. The New Mexico native is best known for playing the sheriff's son, Kyle Valenti, on The WB teen alien hit. Despite *Roswell* being a career-defining opportunity for the young actor, Wechsler disappeared off Hollywood's radar for nearly a decade. "[You have to] strike while the iron's hot and take advantage of this career momentum and all this shit that I just didn't want to do or I didn't do," he said to *TV Line*. "So I made some choices that didn't help me." Wechsler hung on for the next decade, with small roles in films and on television shows like *Malcolm in the Middle* (2003), *Without a Trace* (2007–2008), and *It's Always Sunny in Philadelphia* (2009). But he was frustrated that his time spent on the *Roswell* set hadn't translated into anything substantial. Wechsler's tendency to be extremely hard on himself as

an actor only added to his frustration. "I'm excited about going to work. I love acting," he said. "But I have yet to like one of my own performances." In 2010, Wechsler was close to working with Mike Kelley on *The Quinn-tuplets*, but ended up not getting the part. He didn't make the Kelley connection with *Revenge* until he was at the audition, and he was thrilled by the prospect of working with the *Swingtown* creator. "I wanted to work with Mike Kelley," he told the *Insider*, "but to be honest, there was also a part of me that's just like, 'I need work.'" After years of struggling to make ends meet, it looked like the role of local good guy Jack Porter was the second chance he was waiting for. "The show really took a chance on me."

THE KID BROTHER:
DECLAN PORTER

Thanks to his lifetime of hanging out in Montauk, Jack's made peace with his lot in life. But his younger brother Declan? Not so much. He's ashamed of the "loser" status his family has but, as the season progresses, he comes to appreciate that even though the Porters don't have money, they are rich in love, support, and loyalty. Declan develops from moody teenage brother to being rational and responsible. He'll go to any length to protect his big brother, even so far as perjuring himself on the stand.

Declan's maturity grows as his relationship with Charlotte evolves: at first, he's impressed by her money and status and does everything he can to win her over. Then, when he's with her, he realizes that being a Grayson isn't a blessing but a curse. Finally, as Charlotte becomes everything he can't stand about the wealthy, Declan pulls a 180 in his attitude: he loathes the Graysons, refuses to talk to Charlotte, and does all he can to do right by his own family.

Initially, Declan wants to be more than what his father was, but doesn't understand that the true judge of a man is his character, not his material goods. He's shocked that Charlotte is interested in him and tries to woo her with money made from stolen lobsters and his brother's big, shiny boat. It's only once he realizes that Charlotte wants to be with Declan because of who he is, not what he has, that he relaxes and can be himself around her.

Declan's time with Charlotte is when he matures the most. Once past his desperation to impress her, he shines as he takes care of her, and this confidence extends to his other relationships. He's more tolerant of Jack's decisions and Nolan's presence. He's willing to go to Collins Prep and face the very people who beat him up mere months ago, because he knows that while he may be a "wharf rat" in their eyes, he's special in Charlotte's. And for Declan, that's enough; he can strive for more than his father had, without dishonoring his memory.

Declan was raised to put family first; watching the Grayson family drama unfold underscores for him just how important it is to love and respect the family you have. He's watched Jack sacrifice his dreams for the sake of the Porters, and when he's forced to choose between his family and the girl of his dreams, Declan chooses to protect Jack. It's a decision that the Declan we met on Memorial Day might not have made.

However, there is a major consequence to Declan's family-first policy: his relationship with Charlotte ends. During the later part of the season, Declan nurses his first broken heart. As he develops scar tissue, he also develops certainty about who he is and what matters in life. And that's who stands by you, no matter what, not who has the most money.

THE REAL DEAL
MONTAUK

Jack and Declan are "townies" who live in Montauk, on the south shore of Long Island, about 40 miles from Southampton (where Emily, the Graysons, and Nolan live). With a population of approximately 4,000, Montauk is considered a beach resort town and is the home to many restaurants, bars, and hotels. Considering its distance from Southampton and its reputation as a tourist destination, it's surprising — but not impossible — that Nolan, Emily, and the rest of the resident 1% spend so much time at the Stowaway.

© MP126 / MEDIAPUNCH INC.

CONNOR PAOLO
AS DECLAN PORTER

Connor Paolo (b. July 11, 1990) might be the cast member most familiar with *Revenge*'s depiction of the scandalous lives of Manhattan's elite. He's a born-and-bred New Yorker, and he also honed his craft on a NYC-set show: *Gossip Girl* (2007–2011). For four seasons, he played Eric, Serena van der Woodsen's levelheaded younger brother. While Eric and Declan come from different income brackets — and different worlds — Paolo, the son of a musician father and writer mother, is happy with the move. "It's a new chapter now and I try never to look back," Paolo told the *TV Addict*. "I'm really in love with this character and I'm happy to be here."

Paolo's career began long before he was living at the Palace Hotel. The Professional Performing Arts School graduate (the school made famous by *Fame!*) got his start at nine years old, when he landed a role on the ABC soap *All My Children*. A recurring role on *One Life to Live* followed, and he made his film debut in 2003 in Clint Eastwood's *Mystic River* (2003). Films like *Alexander* (2004) and *World Trade Centre* (2006) followed. Between film gigs, Paolo took to the stage, appearing in the Broadway hit *The Full Monty*. While Paolo was gaining critical acclaim with *GG*, he felt he wasn't ready to commit to TV full-time — until *Revenge* came along. Paolo thought the project was special, and he's glad that fans feel that same way. "If we can make anybody feel good, then we're doing our jobs," he said to *MSN TV*, "and that's a wonderful thing."

the problems

When Emily Thorne carefully planned her Hamptons subterfuge, she could never have anticipated the whole slew of obstacles who would block her path, each with an agenda of their own in hand — and just as willing as Emily to get what they want.

THE MAN WHO KNEW TOO MUCH:
FRANK STEVENS

Frank Stevens makes a living lurking, seeing what others don't, and that's what made his own downfall so shocking: he didn't see it coming.

When we first meet Frank, he's a loyal, dedicated employee, doing whatever dirty deeds Conrad and Victoria ask him to do. But he has a weak spot: Victoria. He protects her reputation when he kills Roger Halsted. But he also protects her heart when he keeps Conrad and Lydia's affair from her. Sure, keeping the secret means he is doing his job as Conrad's head of security. But Frank later tells Victoria about the $10

million in hush money Conrad sent Lydia's way — showing that while Conrad may be Frank's employer, Victoria is his boss.

When putting Victoria ahead of his job gets him fired, Frank decides it's time to go after what he wants. Unemployed and seemingly alone, he has nothing left to lose. But even in this moment of desperation, he shows restraint and an understanding of the power structure in the Hamptons, letting Victoria know what he wants but asking her to make the next move.

As much as Frank wants Victoria, Victoria is the one with the power. She gets to choose who to let into her social circle — and her heart. Frank understands and respects that: despite their differences in social status, Frank and Victoria have a lot in common. They both have shady pasts, dark secrets, and loose morality when it comes to getting the job done.

Frank has a lot in common with Emily too. Frank, like Emily, is driven by a sense of duty and loyalty, and both put their mission ahead of everything else, including their hearts. Both are observant, unflappable, and always have a plan.

But Frank is a warning sign for Emily and for the *Revenge* audience. Frank's loyalty blinds him to warning signs and puts him in harm's way in the service of someone he loves. If Emily continues to do the same, she might meet the same fate as Frank. And it's through Frank, we learn just how fragile Emily's plan is and that the Graysons are more dangerous than they first appear. Why else would they employ a security czar with a willingness to kill to get the job done?

Emily got lucky with Frank. If she catches the eye of someone else as stealthy as him, she could be in big trouble.

 ## MAX MARTINI AS FRANK STEVENS

Max Martini (b. December 11, 1969) has built a career out of acting tough. He's played a military officer in the film *Saving Private Ryan* (1999) and the television series *The Unit* (2006–2009), an FBI agent on *24* (2003), and a DEA agent on *CSI: Miami* (2003–2005). But the tough guy persona isn't just an act. Martini turned to acting after an injury prevented him from playing professional football, and these days the American, Italian, and Canadian citizen keeps fit with mixed martial arts.

THE BACKSTABBING BESTIE:
ASHLEY DAVENPORT

"You're right. I just want your money." With one flip comment in the *Revenge* pilot, Ashley Davenport lays everything on the table for the viewer. She's British, she's poor (or at least not rich), and she wants to be one of New York's elite — not an elite party planner. Despite being clear from the beginning about what she wants, it takes time for Ashley's inner ambitions to be put into action. Does she have what it takes to go after what she wants? And if she does, what is she waiting for?

Ashley experiences three major phases in the first season of *Revenge*. First, she's Emily's loyal friend, showing her the ropes of the Hamptons social scene. Then, she's Tyler's ambitious but cautious girlfriend. Finally, she's the go-get-'em ruthless corporate-ladder climber. Her lack of progress with Emily leads her to lean on Tyler and use his ambition to move forward. But when Tyler begins to unravel, leaving Ashley in his wake, she realizes that she can't rely on anyone to get what she wants. Not a rich best friend, not an influential employer, and not an ambitious boyfriend. The only person she can rely on is herself. So she begins to create opportunities for herself at the expense of others.

She may think she's cunning, but Ashley is rather transparent. Both Daniel's lawyer, Benjamin Brooks, and Conrad Grayson see what she's up to and point it out to her within days of working with her. Nolan figures out pretty quickly that she leaked the photos of Daniel bloodied on the beach. Yet the women she sees and works closely with every day, Emily and Victoria, are clueless. With the social lines clearly drawn, Emily sees her as a friend and Victoria sees her as the help.

If Emily and Victoria were less focused on their own problems and more observant about those around them, maybe they'd see Ashley's ambition and desperation as well as the men around her do. As the season progresses, Ashley shifts from targeting the women — kissing up to Victoria and befriending Emily — to the men — dating Tyler, working for Conrad, and conspiring with Daniel. What this demonstrates is that, despite the battle royale between Emily and Victoria, the men are still very much in charge in the Hamptons. Victoria owes her status in the Hamptons to Conrad. Charlotte's self-worth is defined by her father's identity. Emily's life mission is avenging her father.

While *Revenge* is a show centered on women, these women live in a man's world. And Ashley will do whatever it takes to get to the top.

THE REAL DEAL
CROYDON

With her "population: no one cares and dropping" comment, Ashley Davenport makes her U.K. home, Croydon, sound like a middle-of-nowhere, dead-end small town. Not true. Home to 330,000 people, Croydon is part of the Greater London Area. Its economy used to be largely based on manufacturing, but is now driven by the retail and service industries. Croydon is the birthplace of supermodel Kate Moss — which is why Ashley Madekwe suggested it as her character's hometown when the writers asked her to pick a London suburb for her character to hail from.

 **ASHLEY MADEKWE
AS ASHLEY DAVENPORT**

A student of acting since the age 11, Ashley Davenport (b. December 6, 1981) kicked off her career with the TV movie *Storm Damage* (2000). The London, U.K., native continued her studies at the Royal Academy

78   best served cold

for the Dramatic Arts and the London Academy of Music and Dramatic Art before landing a role in Woody Allen's film *Cassandra's Dream* (2007). However, her big break came in television when she was cast as Bambi, a naïve hooker, in the U.K. series the *Secret Diary of a Call Girl* (2008–2010). When the American cable network Showtime picked up the series, Madekwe became a familiar face across the pond. This success helped her land her first American TV gig, playing a model on The CW show *The Beautiful Life: TBL* (2009). While the show lasted only two episodes, Madekwe met Mike Kelley on the set of *TBL*, and he later offered her the part of Ashley Davenport on *Revenge*.

Madekwe knows that Ashley is one of the characters fans love to hate, but she doesn't mind. In fact, she revels in it. "Everyone on the show takes great relish in playing a scene a little bit 'evil,'" she told *Bello* magazine. "And if people want Ashley to die, then I must be playing the 'evil' right!"

THE TALENTED MR. HAMPTONS:
TYLER BARROL

When Ashton Holmes was asked to sum up his character, he told the *Insider*, "Tyler wants power, and I think he sees Daniel as a way to get that power." This, in essence, is what *Revenge* is all about. Everyone, not just Tyler, wants power. And if they have power, they want to keep it.

While the Hamptonites are all willing to go to extremes to make that happen, Tyler stands out from the other power-hungry characters. As Tyler becomes more unhinged, he gets more brazen about what he wants and sloppier about how he goes after it.

Tyler's obsession with acquiring power starts simply. Daniel represents all that he wants and no longer has, and as Tyler gets closer to Daniel, he realizes how easily he can manipulate the trusting young Grayson. Tyler wants to be the puppet master, and he recognizes that same instinct in Emily, which is why her relationship with Daniel is such a threat to him early on. For Tyler, Daniel represents the key to the Grayson kingdom and whoever controls Daniel has the power.

What makes Tyler's journey unique is his illness. The more he learns about the Graysons and the more he feels his potential future has been unfairly wrenched away from him, the angrier he gets. Combine this with the lack of antipsychotic medication (and, mind you, *Revenge* plays Tyler's downward spiral to dramatic extremes), and the result is one angry, out-of-control fellow that you wouldn't want to run into in a dark alley.

Tyler was on Clozapine, an antipsychotic drug used to treat schizophrenia, usually when other treatment methods have failed. Though Tyler clearly goes crazy after he goes off the medication, he doesn't exhibit the textbook symptoms of schizophrenia. Realism aside, Tyler's psychotic episode shows how well Emily is hiding in plain sight. To see, feel, and believe this girl is out to get the Graysons — and find *just* enough evidence to support your case — would make even the sanest person a little crazy. (See: Victoria Grayson.) But for someone like Tyler, it only enhances his symptoms, driving him closer and closer to the truth — but also over the edge.

The desire for money, power, and privilege isn't the root cause of Tyler's distress. The desire to belong is. He used to be a Daniel Grayson type. He had the family, the money, and the education. Then it was suddenly taken away from him when his family lost everything in the economic collapse. He's frustrated: why does Daniel get to have it all and not him? His downfall wouldn't have been so hard if his family had been by his side — but when the going got really rough, they abandoned him. When you add this to the pile of Tyler's problems, it's easier to understand why he's so angry, why he's jealous of Daniel, and why he hates Emily.

Tyler's understanding of acute loneliness and rejection makes him an effective hustler. He uses his personal experience to create a (false) connection with others, targeting their individual weaknesses. Daniel wants people to understand him for who he is. Ashley wants status and money. Nolan wants companionship. Fauxmanda wants a friend who will tell her the truth. Tyler recognizes each need and, like a good con man, uses it to his advantage.

This is how Tyler figures out Emily's game. Her generic girl-next-door

façade is blemish-free. Emily planned it that way so she could slip into Hamptons society unnoticed, but you can't con a con. Tyler, like Victoria, knows nothing is that perfect. Everyone has problems. Everyone has weaknesses. So when someone as astute as Tyler comes along, Emily's blonde billionaire blandness is a big red warning sign.

ASHTON HOLMES AS TYLER BARROL

Ashton Holmes (b. February 17, 1978) is best known to TV audiences as Sid Phillips from the HBO miniseries *The Pacific* (2010) or as Thorn on The CW's *Nikita* (2010–2011). But the film, stage, and screen actor had been working for over a decade before he made a splash in the Hamptons. *Revenge* was a bit of a homecoming for the Albany, New York, native: his first-ever role was on ABC's daytime soap *One Life to Live* (2002–2003). For the next few years, Holmes paid the bills with small parts in films like *A History of Violence* (2005), *Peaceful Warrior* (2006), and *Smart People* (2008) and with guest spots on TV shows like *Law & Order: Special Victims Unit* (2003), *Ghost Whisperer* (2005), *Boston Legal* (2006), and *House* (2009).

Even though Holmes' run on *Revenge* ended fatally for his character, he loved every second of it. Playing the bad guy is "so freeing as an actor, especially on a soapy drama like *Revenge* where the writing is really fun to perform," he told the *Insider*. "People are coming up to me like, 'Aw, you prick!' Which is so cool."

THE SINGLE WHITE FEMALE:
"AMANDA CLARKE"

A woman of many names — Emily Thorne, Amanda Clarke, Kara Wilkins — Fauxmanda shares one simple desire with so many of the other *Revenge* characters: she just wants to belong.

As she takes on each new identity, Fauxmanda becomes bolder and further separates herself from Emily and what Emily wants for her. As Emily's nameless mysterious friend, she's desperate to prove she belongs with Emily and will do anything to convince her to let her stay. But as Emily pushes her away (claiming it's for her own safety), Fauxmanda looks elsewhere to get what she wants. As Kara Wilkins, she gains the strength to figure this out and it shows in her early flirtations with Jack and defiance of Emily. If Emily won't give her what she wants, Fauxmanda will go out and get it herself elsewhere. And finally, as Amanda Clarke, she's confident: she knows what she wants, does what she wants, and refuses to let go of those she loves. She let go of Emily once — and look where that got her. She won't make the same mistake again, with Emily or with Jack.

Fauxmanda's attachment to Emily isn't fueled by those hefty checks she gets, but by her deep love for her. When they met in juvie, all Fauxmanda needed was a friend, someone to trust and someone to count on. Young Amanda Clarke took advantage of that, seeing in the young Emily Thorne someone she could control and use. Fauxmanda was willing to change names, go on the run, and become the daughter of a nationally hated terrorist because the one person she considered home asked her to. But this devotion and Emily's continued manipulation of her has unintended and complicated consequences. Not only does Emily feel protective of her unpredictable friend who she's created, the friend keeps coming back for more.

Fauxmanda's neediness fuels her attraction to Jack: he's already in love with Amanda Clarke. Amanda was a happy child, with a loving father, a best friend, and a place to call home; Fauxmanda had none of those things. And even though all of that was taken from Amanda, Fauxmanda holds on to the idea that by being Amanda Clarke now, she can have her idyllic life. For the longest time, Emily represented home to Fauxmanda; the two shared a difficult experience and an incredible secret. But now Fauxmanda has the opportunity to build an even more appealing life with someone who doesn't ask insane things of her, who returns affection willingly and openly.

While everyone else in the Hamptons is restrained, Fauxmanda stands

out: she's a firecracker, driven by reckless emotion. She hastily kills Frank because she's scared. She won't get on the plane to Paris. She believes what Emily tells her, then she doesn't. She does what Emily wants, then the opposite. She believes what Tyler tells her, then she doesn't. She's snarky, sassy, and completely off-balance. In many ways, she's Emily's opposite. She oozes sexuality; Emily is restrained. She moves freely; Emily is robotic. She makes decisions with her heart; Emily makes decisions with her head.

Fauxmanda's return to the Hamptons, with a baby on the way, is profound and devastating: not only does this pregnancy have an immediate effect on Emily's (finally) budding romance with Jack, it distances Emily from Fauxmanda. A baby would give Fauxmanda someone to love unconditionally, a connection Emily couldn't give her. But, most importantly, Fauxmanda knows the truth about Emily and she's no longer on Emily's side. She's finally looking out for someone other than Emily: herself.

MARGARITA LEVIEVA AS "AMANDA CLARKE"

Like her *Revenge* character, Margarita Levieva (b. February 9, 1980) has lived many lives. She was born in the Soviet Union, where Levieva trained — hard — to be a gymnast. When Levieva was 11 years old, her family immigrated (illegally) to New York City where she continued to train and compete. She was a state champion and qualified for the U.S. Olympic team, but was unable to attend because she wasn't a legal resident. With her gymnastics career behind her, Levieva enrolled in economics at New York University and began to think about working in business, despite her long-time love of performing. "My family sacrificed a lot to bring me here, and I just felt like I owed something to them, to do something serious in my life," she said to *Under the Radar*. After graduation, she worked briefly as a fashion buyer before giving acting a shot. Her first role was in the 2004 film *Billy's Choice*. Films like *Spread* (2009) and *Adventureland* (2009) followed, but Levieva quickly learned that her strength was in television. After landing a starring role in the short-lived series *Vanished* (2006), she went on to act in the HBO series *How to Make It in America* (2010–2011) before finding her way to the Hamptons. Levieva read the *Revenge* pilot script early on (but never auditioned for any of the roles) and knew the show was special. The *Revenge* team felt the same way about her, and when the role of Emily Thorne's juvie roommate came up, they offered the part to Levieva, no questions asked. Levieva was thrilled. "[My character's] had a hard life and she's got a lot of coping to do," she said to Ology.com. But Levieva is up for the challenge. "My part definitely has an edge."

episode guide

CAST Madeleine Stowe (Victoria Grayson), Emily VanCamp (Amanda Clarke/Emily Thorne), Gabriel Mann (Nolan Ross), Henry Czerny (Conrad Grayson), Ashley Madekwe (Ashley Davenport), Nick Wechsler (Jack Porter), Josh Bowman (Daniel Grayson), Connor Paolo (Declan Porter), Christa B. Allen (Charlotte Grayson)

RECURRING CAST Roger Bart (Mason Treadwell), Ashton Holmes (Tyler Barrol), Margarita Levieva (Emily Thorne/Amanda Clarke), Emily Alyn Lind (Young Amanda), Max Martini (Frank Stevens), James Morrison (White-Haired Man), Derek Ray (Lee Moran), Hiroyuki Sanada (Satoshi Takeda), Nicholas Stargel (Young Jack), James Tupper (David Clarke), Amber Valletta (Lydia Davis)

"When everything you love has been stolen from you, sometimes all you have left is revenge."

1.01 PILOT

AIRED September 21, 2011
WRITTEN BY Mike Kelley
DIRECTED BY Phillip Noyce

Amanda Clarke, now known as Emily Thorne, is back in the Hamptons and it's time for the powerful Grayson family and their fellow conspirators to pay for framing her father for a deadly airplane crash. Her first target: Victoria's best friend and Conrad's mistress, Lydia Davis.

Revenge hits the ground running in its first episode and wastes no time serving up backstory, plot twists, and drop-dead gorgeous Southampton scenery. But appearances can be deceiving. Lurking under that sun-kissed landscape are dark secrets, and the pretty new girl in town is actually a badass hell-bent on vengeance. Beneath Amanda Clarke's — oops, make that Emily Thorne's — girl-next-door façade, her blood runs ice cold. If that wasn't evident from her chilling stares, Lydia's subtext-laden remark about her dip in the freezing ocean water clears that right up.

The very first scene is this episode's most important one. By setting the stage months into the future, viewers know what's coming and what the show is planning to build toward. Who are these people? Who was shot? Emily is marrying Daniel? Why is she mad at Nolan? Why is she best friends with a party planner? In time, all these questions will be answered and the suspense of knowing these revelations are coming makes watching it unfold a hell of a lot more fun. The party scene also introduces an important storytelling element: the flashforward and flashback. This temporal jumping provides insight into what's happening in the present and lets viewers in on a secret or two, enhancing *Revenge's* noir feeling.

The premiere also sets the jam-packed storytelling pace for the rest of the season. The arc of the first half of the season is put into motion, but there's also a self-contained story within the episode: Emily's take-down of Lydia Davis. Accomplishing this within days of her arrival to the Hamptons proves Emily is a woman on a mission.

Thanks to her perjurious testimony against David Clarke, Lydia went from secretary to socialite, and this social status is the very thing Lydia loses when Emily is done with her. Even though Lydia's testimony was devastating to Emily's father, Lydia is just a pawn. Emily has her eyes on a bigger target (if you couldn't tell from her slow-motion pointed stares): Lydia's best friend, Victoria. By taking out Lydia, Emily can capitalize on two of Victoria's biggest weaknesses: her loneliness and her inability to trust. Victoria may seem like she has it all, but it's an illusion. Victoria's empire rests on the public image of her family and her social standing, and she refuses to let anything compromise this power or status, including her best friend. Little does she know that she wasn't the puppet master of this power play. Emily laid out the board so that shunning Lydia was the only move Queen Victoria could make if she wanted to stay in the game, but the end result is further isolating and weakening both Victoria and Conrad. Well played, Ms. Thorne.

Emily came ready to battle, but she wasn't prepared for the appearance of her childhood sweetheart, Jack Porter, and his family. Jack, his father, Carl, and his brother, Declan, are the anti-Graysons. They don't have the cash or social status or need to impress wealthy clientele. But they are loyal (Jack named his boat after a childhood friend), passionate (they'll do whatever it takes to keep their bar), giving (Jack sells his beloved boat to help his dad), and couldn't care less about public perception (Declan, initially, refuses to give in to the cool kids).

Revenge is about playing with these dualities and exploring how they intersect: the Graysons and the Porters, fire and ice, good and evil, best friend and scorned enemy, "absolute forgiveness or moral vindication." But life, no matter how Emily and Victoria view it, isn't black and white. It's shades of gray.

One of those shadier characters is Nolan Ross, a billionaire tech geek with an unexplained devotion to Emily's disgraced father. Nolan has the potential to be dangerous to Emily's plans because of his insider

© TRAVIS JOURDAIN / PR PHOTOS

knowledge of who she really is. In order for her revenge scheme to work, no one can get in the way. When Emily brushes off Jack's invite, she protects her childhood friend from realizing her carefully guarded secret. When she rejects Nolan's offer to help, she protects her mission. The more people in the know and involved, the more potential for trouble. Nolan wants to have a little fun with the takedown scheme, but Emily is not playing games. She's rejected her father's wish that she be forgiving. She means business — and she's a one-person operation.

Like Victoria, Emily may be surrounded by people but ultimately she operates alone. How far will each of these powerful ladies go in order to get their way? And what will happen if they end up squaring off face-to-face? We're about to find out.

BEST SERVED COLD Emily crossed off Lydia's face like most people cross items off their to-do list. It was oddly satisfying to see her take someone down so quickly and so ruthlessly.

HAMPTONS HOMAGE The South Fork Inn is named after South Fork in the Hamptons, but it is also a nod to the original primetime soap, *Dallas*. The Ewing family lived in a mansion on the Southfork Ranch, just outside Plano, Texas.

WHO'S THAT GUY? James Tupper is a familiar face to ABC fans. Before he made the move to the Hamptons, he played Marin's love interest in *Men in Trees* (2006–2008), Samantha's love interest Owen in *Samantha Who?* (2008), and Dr. Andrew Perkins on *Grey's Anatomy* (2010–2011). Unlike many other cast members, who were cautious when discussing the future of *Revenge* while promoting its premiere, Tupper was confident the show would succeed — and wasn't afraid to let others know. "I saw a little bit of what they'd shot in the beginning before I was hired, and I thought, 'This thing is going to be a hit,'" he told the *Toronto Sun*. "I told my whole family, and they were like, 'You're crazy, whatever.' And it is a hit."

Show business is in Emily Alyn Lind's (Young Amanda) blood. Her father is a director and her mother is an actress. Her two sisters, Natalie and Alyvia, are also budding young actresses. Before *Revenge*, Lind's biggest parts were a recurring role on ABC's *All My Children* (2010), the TV movie *November Christmas* (2010), and playing Shirley Temple in the Leonardo DiCaprio film *J. Edgar* (2011). *Special bonus trivia:* Emily's mom, Barbara Alyn Woods, is best known as Deb Lee on *One Tree Hill* — where she once worked with *Revenge* creator Mike Kelley.

BORROWED FROM THE BOOK Lydia's downfall is based on the very first takedown in *The Count of Monte Cristo*. Fernand Mondego, like Lydia, goes along with someone else's diabolical plan because of the wealth and social status he will gain from it. After Dantès is sent to prison, Fernand marries Dantès' fiancée, Mercédès, and becomes a count. But the good times don't last for Fernand. He is publicly shamed — just like Lydia — after a trial reveals his past crimes. Disgraced and alone, Fernand decides that the only way out is suicide. Victoria uses Lydia's past crimes to socially disgrace her, and Lydia, like Fernand, believes she can't show her face in this world again.

BEHIND THE SCENES James Tupper wasn't supposed to be David Clarke. *Buffy the Vampire Slayer* star Marc Blucas (Buffy's love interest Riley Finn) played David in the original cut of the pilot. But when Mike Kelley decided to expand the role to more than a handful of episodes, Blucas had to drop out. He was already committed to USA's *Necessary Roughness* and an increased *Revenge* workload just wasn't possible. "It was disappointing," Blucas said to *Star News Online*. "I really liked where they wanted that character on *Revenge* to go." But he took the decision in stride. "My hat's off to USA, because I really didn't think they'd be cool with me going out and doing *any* episodes on another network."

Emily threatening to break Nolan's windpipe was a last-minute addition to the script, thanks to director Phillip Noyce. Noyce, fresh off directing the Angelina Jolie action movie *Salt,* wanted Emily Thorne to be more like Jolie's character, Evelyn Salt. To make this happen, he added a martial arts background and surprising physical strength, one more weapon in Emily Thorne's bag of tricks. "He made Emily Thorne more of a badass . . . than I originally imagined her," Kelley said.

REVENGENDA Where will Lydia go now? Will Conrad face Victoria's wrath as Lydia did? Does Daniel get shot on the beach on Labor Day? Why is Jack there? Where did the sand on Emily's hand come from? Did Emily have anything to do with the shooting?

REVENGESPIRATION
"Well, don't let them see your weakness. It's the first thing they use against you." — Victoria Grayson

REVENGE READING
HOMER'S *ODYSSEY*

It doesn't take a tech genius like Nolan Ross to figure out that Sammy is almost 20 years old, a remarkable feat for a golden retriever — they usually live 12 to 15 years. Maybe Sammy is a descendent of Odysseus's dog, Argos.

Odysseus, the protagonist of the epic Greek poem the *Odyssey* — which was penned between 750 and 650 BCE — is a soldier who, after spending 10 years fighting the Trojan War, spends another 10 years trying to return to his home, Ithaca. Along the way, he faces many challenges including battling a Cyclops, a sea monster, a witch, and several sea storms. When he finally returns, he finds his house overrun with greedy ambitious men, who want to marry his wife and who are living off his family's resources and reveling in his presumed death. Despite being 20 years older, battle weary, and in disguise, Odysseus is immediately recognized by Argos, an ever-faithful companion — just as Sammy runs up to Emily the moment he sees her.

There are a lot of similarities between Emily and Odysseus, beyond their respective revenge plans. Like Odysseus, Emily spent nearly 20 years wandering before returning home. They both use smarts rather than strength to defeat their enemies, don disguises to infiltrate and conquer the place they once called home, and only their most faithful canine friends recognize them. Most importantly, both are ruthless when it comes to getting what they want, whether it's revenge or reclaiming what is rightfully theirs.

If Emily is Odysseus, that makes Jack her Penelope, Odysseus's faithful wife, who is certain that her one true love will one day come back home. Jack and Penelope are dignified people who tolerate their entitled visitors, while their closest family members — Penelope's son, Telemachus, and Jack's brother, Declan — can't stand most of them. Penelope is quite manipulative, deceiving her suitors and cleverly testing Odysseus to see if he has really come home at last. Jack, on the other hand, is good-hearted but shows no innate cunning. But as the clues pile up, it may be only a matter of time before Jack, like Penelope, puts two and two together and figures out who Emily really is.

What lessons can this Greek myth teach Emily Thorne? First, that she should plan everything and prepare for anything. In the *Odyssey*, the gods mess with Odysseus's plans at their whim, often using him as a pawn in their personal quibbles, which catches Odysseus by surprise and unravels his plans. Instead of attempting to predict the unexpected, Emily could learn to roll with changes or setbacks, to leverage them to her advantage.

Second, Emily should know that nothing is as simple as it seems. Odysseus may be the hero, but he's far from a saint. He's a liar and a murderer and wasn't entirely faithful to his wife and family when he was away. Similarly, not all of the suitors are pure evil: some treat Penelope and the memory of Odysseus with respect. Yet good or bad, all the suitors suffer the same terrible fate. The world of the *Odyssey*, like that of *Revenge*, can't be easily divided into black and white, right and wrong, or good and evil.

Emily may think she is entitled to her revenge, but as the *Odyssey* shows us, that doesn't mean that the journey to her Ithaca will be easy. She's going to have to earn it.

●　●　●

"In the end the only person we can truly trust is ourselves."

1.02 TRUST

AIRED September 28, 2011
WRITTEN BY Mike Kelley and Joe Fazzio
DIRECTED BY Phillip Noyce

Emily grows closer to Daniel and takes down another target: hedge-fund manager and former family friend Bill Harmon.

The second episode kicks off *Revenge*'s trademark "theme of the week" format and this time, Emily is focused on trust. Or, as the case may be, lack of trust. Emily doesn't trust anyone, but she might need to make exceptions if she wants to move ahead with her game plan. If it weren't for Nolan, she wouldn't have scored her coveted revenge headquarters, her childhood beach house.

Choosing who to trust can be a gamble. You can never be certain if someone is playing by the same rules — or even the same game — as you.

Emily knows this and it's reflected in her cautious, ruthless nature. There was a ton of game imagery throughout this episode — Bill Harmon is constantly fiddling with dice; Emily meets Bill by agreeing to wager on a polo match; and the dialogue is rife with game analogies — designed to reinforce the game-playing going on between Emily and her targets and to demonstrate what a gamble Emily is taking with her vendetta.

Emily's lack of trust compensates for her father's overly trusting nature. David Clarke confided in Bill about his relationship with Victoria, and Bill burned him with the frame job. But, as the *Revenge* tagline assures us, what goes around comes around. Bill decides to trust Emily's carefully crafted persona without a background check or portfolio transfer, and it causes his downfall. He rolls the dice when it comes to trusting her. Emily uses Bill's past willingness to make cash off illegal insider trading to set a trap she knows he'll walk right into. She rolls the dice herself, believing he'll bet big on her faux inside tip from Nolan.

With the confidence of the uber privileged, Daniel is also quick to trust. When you've never wanted for anything, trusting is easy. He trusts his place in the world, as a wealthy soon-to-be graduate of Harvard who will be handed the reins of Grayson Global one day. He trusts that his meddling mother and distant father only have his best interests at heart. He trusts his feelings about Emily and that their relationship is strong enough already to warrant a surprise house party, unwittingly throwing her a party on her birthday. Being an open guy, Daniel assumes that, like him, Emily would love a surprise party and he has no problem filling her house with friends. But Emily is *not* a fan of surprises and would prefer to celebrate in isolation. The poignant sadness of her solo cupcake and whispered "Happy birthday, Amanda" is the icing on the cake.

Another less-trusting soul is Jack Porter. Jack is troubled by Nolan's generosity; the billionaire seems to be playing a game of his own and Jack doesn't know the rules. When you can buy anything you want or need, there's less risk and more fun in gambling. But when life deals you a less lucrative hand than Daniel or Nolan, and you've struggled and scraped for every dime, you've learned that gambling — especially when it comes to who you trust — is dangerous. Jack doesn't trust Nolan's intentions or his money. However, if Jack wants his family's business to survive, he'll need to trust those who want to lend a hand, including Nolan.

Emily is in the same boat. If she wants her revenge rampage to move forward, she has to trust *someone*. Emily needs Nolan's techie expertise, but she also wants someone to share her victories with. It's no fun winning when you're playing alone. She downplays showing Nolan the news clip about Harmon's financial ruin as a simple FYI, but the glee on her face reveals that she's proud and wants to share it with someone. Even lone wolf Victoria entrusts someone to do her dirty work. Frank may have kept Conrad and Lydia's affair from her, but Victoria choses to trust him, though she doesn't trust her new next-door neighbor . . . or anyone else.

Trusting someone is a gamble: if you trust too much, you might get burned; if you don't trust anyone, you might end up alone. But what this episode demonstrates is that the best way to play isn't to choose one extreme or the other. It's about deciding who you want on your team — and when you want to roll the dice.

BEST SERVED COLD On the menu at afternoon tea at the Graysons' is tea, scones, and a healthy serving of backhanded compliments, iced in layers of contempt. No one delivers an evil eye quite like Madeleine Stowe, but Emily VanCamp held her own in this showdown.

HAMPTONS HOMAGE Daniel quotes Oliver Wendell Holmes Sr. (1809–1894) to Emily after their date: "Where we love is home, home that our feet may leave, but not our hearts." Wendell Holmes, a poet and physicist, is considered one of the most conventional of America's most famous poets; Daniel's association with him reinforces the idea that he's an all-American good guy and a conventional romantic prospect.

When Bill Harmon shows Emily his stock profile, he tells her it's "for your eyes only." "For Your Eyes Only" was a James Bond 1960 short story (and 1981 film) about a young woman seeking to avenge her parents' murders who succeeds with the help of Bond.

WHO'S THAT GUY? When Matthew Glave (Bill Harmon) is on

television, he's usually playing a good guy, not a bad guy. The Michigan native is best known to television audiences as Deputy Bud Skeeter from *Picket Fences* (1995–1996), Dr. Dale Edson from *ER* (1996–2002), and Lt. Colonel Evan Connors from *Army Wives* (2008–2009).

BORROWED FROM THE BOOK The Bill Harmon storyline is a re-imagining of Dantès' takedown of Baron Danglars, the man who came up with the idea to frame Dantès. Like Harmon, Danglars is a wealthy financier who used inside information to take advantage of the market. Dantès sends a message to Danglars with false information about the current political climate, causing him to make a few bad bets and lose everything. The big difference between the two takedowns is that Dantès uses telegrams, so Danglars never knows that the wrong information came from him, but Emily feeds Harmon the bad tip face-to-face.

BEHIND THE SCENES Josh Bowman managed to bring a bit of British royalty to his portrayal of the Hamptons prince. He draws inspiration for Daniel from the U.K.'s hard-partying Prince Harry, as well as the late John F. Kennedy Jr., who may be Harry's closest American counterpart.

When Bowman moved to this side of the pond, he signed up for weekly lessons to perfect his American accent. Bowman treats learning a new accent like learning a new piece of music. "You want to find the rhythm and the melody," he said. "Some notes you hit wrong." After years of practice, Bowman now has it down pat, but he struggles in scenes opposite fellow Brit Ashley Madekwe. "When I hear her accent, I think, 'Oh, I'm home.' But I'm not," he told *Good Morning America*.

REVENGENDA Is Emily really falling for Daniel, or is it all part of her master plan? Why does Nolan keep bringing Jack into Emily's orbit, when it's clear she wants Jack far, far away? What card does Lydia have up her sleeve?

REVENGESPIRATION
"The worst betrayals come from those we trust the most." — David Clarke

ON LOCATION
FILMING *REVENGE*

The Hamptons is where New York City's rich and famous party their summer holidays away. It's also where *Revenge* is set. However, despite those glorious shots of beautiful beaches, delightful downtowns, and magnificent marinas, it's not where *Revenge* is filmed. In fact, several cast members (including stars Emily VanCamp and Madeleine Stowe) and show creator, Mike Kelley, had never set foot in the Hamptons until *Revenge* was well under way. So how does the *Revenge* production crew re-create the iconic beachfront town week in and week out? With a little Hollywood magic and a great big green screen.

For John Hansen, who served as *Revenge*'s production designer for the show's early episodes, including the pilot, it was important to get the Hamptons vibe just right: "For me the essence of the Hamptons is like walking into a Norman Rockwell painting or an Edward Hopper painting. It's that quintessential Americana small town." The *Revenge* pilot was shot in such a place: Wilmington, North Carolina (the same seaside community where The WB's *Dawson's Creek* was filmed). With smart location selection and by mimicking architectural elements traditionally found in the Hamptons, Hansen and location manager Chris Campbell found acceptable stand-ins in North Carolina for all the major locations in *Revenge*. Scenes inside Emily's and Victoria's homes were filmed in houses near Wilmington. The beach scenes were filmed on nearby Oak Island, the Memorial Day party took place on a local riverboat, and the ER scenes were filmed in the neighborhood hospital. Even the ship that became the *Amanda* was originally found in Wilmington. Scenes in the Stowaway were filmed in Fishy Fishy, a local café in nearby Southport.

The café, a bright and cheerful restaurant, was undergoing major renovations at the time. When the *Revenge* location scouts came calling in the winter of 2011, Marci Phillips, Fishy Fishy's owner, put the renos on hold and jumped at the chance to be involved in the show. The entire process — turning Fishy Fishy into a dark tavern, filming the Stowaway scenes, and returning the restaurant back to its original state — took merely four days of "around the clock" work, Phillips said. Furniture, window coverings, and even light fixtures were changed to create Montauk's "local treasure." Phillips said the process was "exhilarating but exhausting" and would jump at the chance to do it again. "What goes into setting up for a TV pilot just blew me away," she said. "It was a wonderfully positive experience."

The cast and crew agreed and felt Wilmington's natural beauty paid tribute to what the show was trying to accomplish. "Wilmington is beautiful," Emily VanCamp said to *Star News Online*. "It lent itself beautifully to turn into the Hamptons."

It was important to get Grayson Manor and Emily Thorne's beach house just right. Victoria is queen of the Hamptons and her giant home, complete with the menacing balcony where she can watch over her kingdom, is essential to creating this powerful, but lonely, character who reigns over a dysfunctional, drama-prone family. The home, like Victoria, needed to be elegant, exquisitely decorated, and cold. The scenes in Victoria's house in the pilot were shot in a home in Landfall, a wealthy community next to Wilmington; the production crew kept the stunning house as-is for filming *Revenge*,

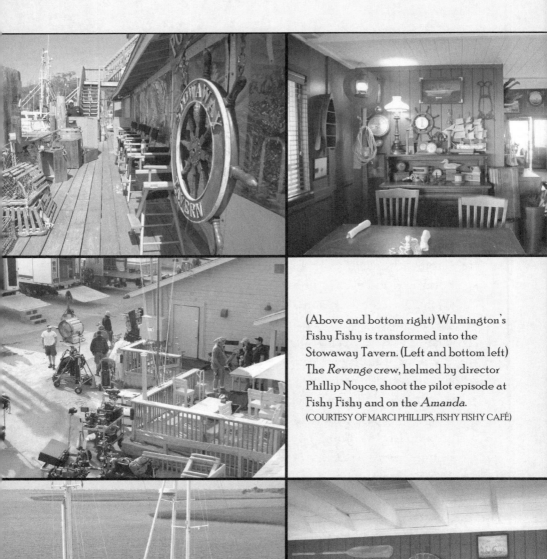

(Above and bottom right) Wilmington's Fishy Fishy is transformed into the Stowaway Tavern. (Left and bottom left) The *Revenge* crew, helmed by director Phillip Noyce, shoot the pilot episode at Fishy Fishy and on the *Amanda*. (COURTESY OF MARCI PHILLIPS, FISHY FISHY CAFÉ)

furniture and all. However, the expansive exterior of the 24,000-square-foot Grayson Manor was more difficult to create. It's beautiful but, sadly, it's fake. The exteriors are modeled on a real East Hampton home (which isn't an oceanfront residence), but even that mansion wasn't grand enough for the Graysons. *Revenge*'s production team gave it a digital remodeling: they stretched the length of the house, moved the pool to the front of the property, added the turret where Victoria's balcony sits, and placed the house directly on the waterfront, because a family like the Graysons wouldn't be satisfied with anything less than a million-dollar view.

If you prefer Emily's beach house, head to North Carolina. The homes used for the interior and exterior are both in Wilmington. Inside and out, the beach house reflects Emily's public image as the charming girl next door. It's casual and homey, but refined and tasteful.

When ABC picked up *Revenge*, all three major locations were re-created at the Raleigh Studios in Manhattan Beach, California, where the rest of the first season was filmed. Nolan's sleek and modern home, first seen in "Betrayal," is a beachfront property in Malibu, California, that's regularly used on television (including The CW's *90210*). It was a smart choice for this forward-thinking socially inept billionaire, as it reflects the characteristics that made him rich and it contrasts nicely with the older-money manors.

The set designers replicated the interior of the original houses (even duplicating most of the furniture used in the original Grayson Manor), but with a keen eye, you'll notice a few differences between the pilot and the subsequent episodes. In Emily's home, the structural beams are in different places and the walls are pale green, whereas in the pilot they were white. In the pilot, some of Emily's porch is screened in; when we return to that porch in the second episode, it's not. There were changes to the Grayson home as well. Victoria's couches in the living room are different, and there's suddenly a staircase opening into the living room. But, hey, these people are wealthy. Maybe they just commissioned some quickie renovations between episodes.

As important as the houses are to understanding the characters on *Revenge*, "the most iconic landmark in the Hamptons is the beach," Campbell said. Each episode of *Revenge* is complemented with aerial shots and beach views shot by a crew sent to the Hamptons, and this footage is added to each scene in post-production. "We can place the beach, we can place the ocean, we can place the harbor right off our set so you can feel like you're on the east coast," Hansen explained. Those beautiful overhead and seaside shots are, in fact, bona fide Hamptons landscape. However, these green-screened backgrounds make scenes feel glossy and artificial, as if *Revenge* takes place in an alternate world; things feel just a little bit off and you can't put your finger on why. This meta quality is intentional, according to *Revenge* creator Mike Kelley, as it reflects the entire premise of the show. "Something doesn't feel quite right, but it's still beautiful to look at," Kelley said to the *Daily Beast*. "We like keeping the viewer trapped in our world. There's something about it that feels magical and distant, and a little bit spooky."

●　●　●

*"For the innocent, the past might hold a reward.
But for the treacherous, it's only a matter of time before the past
delivers what they truly deserve."*

1.03 BETRAYAL

AIRED October 5, 2011
WRITTEN BY Salvatore Stabile
DIRECTED BY Matt Earl Beesley

Victoria tries to uncover Emily's past, while Daniel is forced to face his own. Meanwhile, his best friend from Harvard arrives in town, and so does Emily's latest target: Senator Tom Kingsly.

The third episode of *Revenge* focuses on one of the show's biggest themes: betrayal. Emily wouldn't be here in the first place if people hadn't betrayed her father. Tom Kingsly, the prosecutor-turned-senator, is one of the many who turned on Emily's father. But he also betrayed his family, his political beliefs, and his mistress, making him an easy target on Emily's hit list. Like Lydia Davis and Bill Harmon previously, Emily uses his own mistakes and bad decisions against him by uncovering them for all to see and letting the chips fall where they may.

Yet, if the dream that opens the episode suggests anything, it's that Emily isn't the cool cucumber she appears to be. She's scared of being exposed, of being taken away just like her father was years ago. And with Victoria and Frank circling like sharks, it's with good reason. She also has a heart buried beneath that cold exterior. While Emily has an ulterior motive for exposing Daniel to his ex-girlfriend's brother (to further drive a wedge between Daniel and Victoria), her response to his confession demonstrates that she's far from unfeeling. That emotional response would be pretty damn difficult (and impressive) to fake. She's beginning to see Daniel as a person — one who owns up to his mistakes — and not just as the son of those who wronged her father and benefits from their ill-gotten gains. Daniel, despite his crazy family and personal flaws, is proving to be an upstanding, considerate guy who regrets his past and is keen to do the right thing. Is Emily responding to his sweetness, openness, and honesty or beginning to feel bad that, in the end, she's going to have to take him down?

Adam betrays Charlotte when he hooks up with the blonde, but Declan decides not to use this betrayal to his advantage. He rises above his destructive feelings and sends Charlotte a sweet video instead. But Declan is fallible; he misses his father's wake and refuses to join Jack to scatter his ashes. In emotional turmoil, he feels terrible about his last interaction with his dad, demonstrating that despite his desire to be better than a bartender, he feels as though he betrayed his father and his family by having those judgmental thoughts.

In Emily's eyes, Victoria committed the biggest betrayal of all: Victoria loved David Clarke. She still thinks about him fondly — as the earring flashback poignantly demonstrates — but she didn't do enough to save him. She had the power and the knowledge to prevent his conviction, but her eleventh-hour appeal to Kingsly failed, and she gave up. Emily knows Victoria's darkest secret and, as a result, is focusing on the queen bee as opposed to her husband. Conrad seems more than willing to cover up misdeeds — he springs into action to help Kingsly do so — and shows no regret over what they did to Clarke. Unlike Conrad, Victoria is torn: she betrays both sides with her conflicting values.

Emily wants Victoria to do what Daniel did: to face her past and own up to her mistakes. Both mother and son destroyed the life of a loved one, but Daniel did so without malicious intent or forethought, then acknowledged his sin and repented. Victoria forbade Daniel from atoning for his mistake; by banning him from seeing his former girlfriend Sarah, she keeps him swimming in guilt like she does. Instead of trying to drive Daniel away from Emily's influence, perhaps Victoria should follow her lead if she wants to finally let go of her past. Daniel feels relief after admitting his wrongdoing. But if the past is any indication it seems when Victoria finally finds her conscience when it comes to David Clarke, it will be too little, too late.

BEST SERVED COLD Emily bought the building that Senator Kingsly's mistress lives in and videotaped her every move inside. Ems is one thorough and a very long-term planner.

HAMPTONS HOMAGE Nolan calls Declan "grasshopper," an often-used reference from the TV series *Kung Fu* (1972–1975), which followed Kwai Chang Caine, a martial arts expert and monk, as he traveled throughout the American West in search of his half-brother. A grasshopper — both the insect and the many students the term now refers to in pop culture — must watch, wait, and learn before making their move, which is what Emily must do if she wants her plan to succeed and Declan must do if he wants to get the girl.

WHO'S THAT GUY? Yancey Arias (Senator Tom Kingsly) may look familiar thanks to his roles in *Kingpin* (2003), *The Division* (2004), *Thief* (2006), and the *Knight Rider* reboot (2008–2009), but the native New Yorker is best known in Hollywood for the role he didn't take. In 2003, Arias was offered the part of Carlos, the husband of Eva Longoria's character Gabrielle Solis, on *Desperate Housewives*, but passed in order to do *Wanted*, a CBS pilot that wasn't picked up.

BORROWED FROM THE BOOK Tom Kinglsy is the modern-day reincarnation of Monsieur de Villefort, *The Count of Monte Cristo*'s ambitious attorney-turned-politician. After sending Dantès to jail as the deputy public prosecutor of Marseille, Villefort goes on to have a successful political career. Villefort strongly defines himself a royalist, just as Kingsly aligns himself with conservative family values. Like Kingsly, Villefort is not a faithful husband. He had an affair with Madame Danglars, which results in an illegitimate child. The prosecutor does his best to cover it up, but when Dantès learns about the affair, he uses this information to end Villefort's political career.

BEHIND THE SCENES Why does Declan have an accent unlike anyone else on the show? It's especially strong in the sweet video he sends Charlotte at the end of this episode. According to Connor Paolo, it's because pilot director Phillip Noyce requested it. Paolo and Nick Wechsler were tasked with researching Montauk accents, and this is what Paolo came up with. "We live in Montauk, which is the end of the island," he explained to *Entertainment Weekly*. "People from Montauk have a strong accent." Wechsler was supposed to do the accent as well, but gave up on it because he found it distracting; he admitted that doing this put Paolo in a weird position. "I screwed him over," he told *Xfinity*. "He's just being a good, hard-working actor, and I am terrible at accents." Thanks to Wechsler's lack of accent, Paolo's feels out of place and he eventually drops it.

REVENGENDA Will Charlotte ever dump Adam for Declan? What are the Porters going to do, with their father gone and the bar in debt? Will Victoria ever get over what she did to David Clarke? And if she does, what happens next?

REVENGESPIRATION
"Violence is only one way to take someone down." — Nolan Ross

MUSIC
ON *REVENGE*

When that haunting piano riff hits the screen, dancing over the image of black waves ready to take you under, you know it's time for *Revenge*. The music on the show helps to elevate *Revenge* from a generic primetime soap to a transportive noir experience, rich with nuance. Viewers have two people to thank for that: conductor and orchestrator Fil Eisler, known professionally as iZLER, and music supervisor Season Kent.

In Prague, Czechoslovakia, iZLER grew up in a musical family. His grandmother worked as a music therapist. "She was huge musical influence on me," iZLER said, and she was part of the reason he joined a choir and signed up for piano lessons at the age of six. As a teen, he moved to England and fell in love with the guitar. He met Robbie Williams and joined his band in 1998, playing bass, guitar, and sometimes drums for the British pop star. After four years of touring, he branched out by starting up his own band and working with other artists like Ryan Adams, Kylie Minogue, and Imogen Heap. But he eventually decided he needed a change — a big one. So he moved to Los Angeles to pursue a long-time dream of his: writing music for movies and television. His TV credits include *ER*, *Studio 60 on the Sunset Strip*, *Thief*, *This Revolution*, and *Shameless*. Mike Kelley and pilot director Phillip Noyce learned about iZLER's work from the 2011 film *On the Ice*. For *Revenge*'s opening theme, Kelley was looking for "something to do with the sea, a simple piano melody," iZLER recalled. The composer promised to come up with something, but when he got home, he realized he already had the perfect piece of music: a composition he had done for a friend's short film. He sent the music to Kelley right away and was hired the following Monday morning.

Revenge's score is recorded with an orchestra, usually consisting of 20 to 30 string instruments, which is extremely unusual for television. (In the season finale, iZLER upped the orchestra to 50 members and included wind instruments and percussion.) However, it is important to iZLER that *Revenge* has this element: "I am all about live music." Noyce and Kelley were open to the idea because an orchestra would best lend itself to the "big and dark" mood they were trying to create. "I knew that I wanted this show to have a bit of the Hitchcock *Psycho* element," iZLER said to *Beatweek*. It works. Whether Emily is telling yet another lie, or leaning in for a kiss from Daniel, the big, swelling score reinforces that things are never as they seem, and that destruction and danger lurk just under the surface.

The other half of *Revenge*'s musical equation, the commercial music, is Season Kent's domain. She's the one who decides what songs should play when in any given episode of *Revenge*. Originally from Tennessee, Kent headed to L.A. after graduating from Middle Tennessee State University. After working on movie soundtracks as an intern, she was hired first as an assistant, then coordinator, where she toiled for five years on the music for films like the Austin Powers series, *Charlie's Angels*, and *Training Day*. She eventually made the shift into music supervision and worked on over 20 films, including the Oscar-nominated movie *The Fighter*, *Dear John*, and *Limitless*. Eventually, she decided to add television to her already impressive résumé and partnered with Clearsongs Inc. It was her relationship with Clearsongs that brought Kent to the set of *Revenge*.

How does Kent choose what music to feature on *Revenge*? Once she establishes the direction of the episode with the producer and director, she gets creative. "My gut instinct always comes into play," she explained to SongDetective.com. Sometimes her gut speaks to her before she's seen tape or chatted with the production team. For example, while putting together the music for the pilot, Kent discovered Danish singer/songwriter Agnes Obel. "Her haunting layered vocals and piano melodies are perfect for Emily." She knew she had to use Obel's music and even knew where: over the montage that closes *Revenge*'s second episode. The team put their trust in Kent and the risk paid off. Obel's song "Avenue" perfectly captures the many elements at play in that episode: the tension building in the Grayson family, the devastation facing the Porters, and Emily's increasingly intent quest for vengeance. Kent is a fan of featuring independent artists, including Obel, noise pop band the Crocodiles, and laid-back Canadian act Bahamas, on the show. Not only are they cheaper to license, but using up-and-comers establishes *Revenge* (and, by association, Kent) as an industry tastemaker.

Since Victoria Grayson is the kind of woman who's always ahead of the game, it's only fitting that the music on her series does the same.

• ● •

"The greatest weapon anyone can use against us is our own mind."

1.04 DUPLICITY

AIRED October 12, 2011
WRITTEN BY Wendy Calhoun
DIRECTED BY Matt Shakman

Emily sets her sights on a fourth target: Dr. Michelle Banks. Meanwhile, grief drives a wedge between Declan and Jack, Tyler drives a wedge between Daniel and Emily, and a stunning revelation drives a wedge between Victoria and Charlotte.

Everyone in the Hamptons, it seems, is deceiving those around them. Banks secretly videotapes her clients. Conrad pretends all is well with his family, yet continues his affair with Lydia. Tyler acts like Daniel's caring bestie, but meddles in his relationship with Emily. Emily preys on those around her while pretending to be the lovely girl next door. Victoria fakes her Hamptons matriarch persona, but underneath battles guilt and regret, including conflicted feelings about Charlotte and their relationship.

Charlotte reacts so strongly to Victoria's taped confession for two reasons. First, hearing that your mother thinks your birth may have been a mistake is a horrible thing to experience. Second, it confirms Charlotte's own doubts that her relationship with her mother isn't what it seems. Of all the secrets Victoria may have revealed to Dr. Banks, it's fitting that Emily chose this one to show at the tea: it preys on Charlotte's shaky status in her family and creates more problems for all the Graysons, not just Victoria.

Charlotte isn't the only Grayson with doubts. Daniel doubts Emily's faithfulness to him and his own ability to change; Victoria doubts Conrad's desire to fix his family; and Conrad doubts Victoria's insistence that she had nothing to do with destroying Kingsly's career. The Grayson façade isn't as convincing as they think it is, and Tyler, Emily, and who knows who else prey on these weaknesses. It's relatively easy and extremely effective strategy.

Once again, the Graysons' hidden turmoil contrasts sharply with the Porters, who wear their hearts on their sleeves. Declan charms Charlotte just by being himself. In a world where she isn't sure about anything, his honest, open demeanor feels as fresh as the salty summer air. Especially after she realizes at the fundraiser tea that any effort to be the daughter her mother wants is for naught, because her mother questions wanting a daughter at all. Declan's family may not have money, privilege, or power, but he can be true to himself — and that's the kind of freedom Charlotte wants. She sees that Declan's mother's ring is priceless to him, though valueless to anyone else. Charlotte wants to experience that depth of feeling, and she takes the first step when she boldly tells her mother she won't pretend to be someone she's not.

Declan encourages Charlotte to let go of the past and do what she can to salvage her future relationship with her mother. Yet Declan can't let go of the past himself, and neither can his brother. Declan can't give up their mother's ring and Jack can't give up their father's bar. As their past defines who they are, they let it determine their future. They aren't alone in doing this: Victoria still struggles with framing David Clarke, Daniel is caught between embracing his party boy past and building a

© TATIANA DAVIDOV / PR PHOTOS

future with Emily, and Emily refuses to contemplate a future that doesn't involve avenging the past.

Speaking of the past, it looks like Dr. Banks's finally caught up with her. Michelle Banks was a regular woman with an average job, until she made a deal with a devil. Emily's first three targets were soapy clichés of the wealthy we've seen before and love to watch go down: the cheating socialite, the corrupt Wall Street broker, and the two-faced politician. When we met them, they were still making bad decisions — Victoria could have found out about Conrad and Lydia somehow; Harmon could have been caught for insider trading eventually; and Kinglsy's mistress might have returned anyway — but Banks's only current mistake is videotaping her clients without their knowledge. However, Banks has the distinction of being the only target (so far) who directly dealt with Emily and had a say in her future, an action which Emily judges to be as damning as the rest. So perhaps the punishment fit the crime when Emily locked Banks in the shipping container as the doctor once locked young Amanda Clarke in a detention cell.

Victoria is in her own prison, one she built out of secrets, deceit, and regret. And she's not the only one. Charlotte and Daniel are imprisoned by the expectations of others, the Porters are imprisoned by familial duty, and Emily is imprisoned by her desire to right the wrongdoings her family suffered. Until they each accept their pasts, they won't be able to move forward — and they won't be free.

BEST SERVED COLD Those Hampton housewives confessions gave any episode of *The Real Housewives* a run for its money. If you want to re-live all the public shaming glory, check out HamptonsExposed.com — it's actually up and running. (Thanks for those clone sites, Nolan!)

HAMPTONS HOMAGE In Emily's therapy session with Dr. Banks, the video camera is hidden on top of a copy of Alexandre Dumas' *The Count of Monte Cristo*.

WHO'S THAT GUY? Amy Landecker (Dr. Michelle Banks) spent 20 years on stage in Chicago before heading to Hollywood. Guest spots on shows like *Law & Order* (2008), *Mad Men* (2008), *Medium* (2009), and *House* (2011) keep her busy, but her most memorable TV turn was playing Louis C.K.'s girlfriend, then his mom, on two different episodes of *Louie* in 2010.

This isn't the first time Cassius Willis (Detective Robert Gunther) suited up to play a crime solver. He's best known for playing Detective Gil Wallace on the CBS daytime soap *The Young and the Restless* (2008–2009).

BORROWED FROM THE BOOK Dantès punishes Danglars one final time by imprisoning him in a cell without food or water. After 12 days of being held, Dantès finally comes to him, reveals his true identity, and forgives Danglars for his crimes. Emily also uses a cell as a form of punishment for Dr. Banks, although she left her locked up for no more than 12 hours, not 12 days.

BEHIND THE SCENES Emily Thorne knows how to give a look that can kill. There's a classic example of it when Emily stops Nolan in the golf cart. On set, this death stare is known as "The Croc." While shooting the pilot, Emily had two sources of inspiration for it: a photo of Grace Kelly emerging from water with a piercing stare and a picture of a crocodile. "It just embodies what I imagined this character to be," she told *Rolling Stone*. "In a very weird way, they looked so similar." Wherever it comes from, it works. A scene with Nolan isn't complete without one and the running joke on set is "we don't stop 'til we get The Croc."

REVENGENDA What, exactly, is Tyler up to? Does Nolan really believe Emily's confession is about Jack, or is he just playing games? Did Victoria bribe Dr. Banks to institutionalize Amanda because Amanda saw her take David's laptop and wanted the truth kept hidden?

REVENGESPIRATION
"People who aren't who they claim to be, Amanda, are very, very dangerous. You would be wise to remember that." — Dr. Michelle Banks

"Guilt is a powerful affliction. You can try to turn your back on it, but that's when it sneaks up behind you and eats you alive."

1.05 GUILT

AIRED October 19, 2011
WRITTEN BY Nikki Toscano
DIRECTED BY Kenneth Fink

Lydia tries to blackmail her way back into the Hamptons, but ends up crushed on a roof of a cab instead. Which bodes well for Emily, as Lydia was determined to unearth Emily's own "Southfork Inn."

Episode five was a game-changer for *Revenge*. Not only did the writers abandon the procedural, takedown-of-the-week format, "Guilt" demonstrates how much havoc Emily's presence has brought to the Hamptons, gives the show its first present-day (attempted?) murder, and (finally!) shows Emily in trouble. In short, shit got real.

The driving force behind Emily's quest for revenge is revealed: it's guilt. For 10 years, she believed her father was a terrorist. Her mission is fueled by her need to right that wrong, to compensate for not believing in him.

What is fueling Lydia, however, is not guilt: she wants her life back. (If she has any guilt at all, it's about ruining her friendship with Victoria.) Money alone isn't enough to satisfy either Lydia or Emily: Emily didn't take her 49% of Nolan's company and run, nor will Lydia leave with Conrad's $10 million. Both these ladies have bigger plans for their buckets of cash. Victoria destroyed their worlds, and they want justice: for Emily, that means wrongs must be righted; for Lydia, her demands include a détente with Victoria, the beach house, and a return to the Grayson inner circle.

While Lydia is terrified of placelessness, Daniel is embracing it. (Although having a billionaire girlfriend probably helps ease the pain of

When everything you love has been stolen
from you, sometimes all you have left is . . .

revenge

"The most dangerous secrets a person can bury are those we keep from ourselves."

IT'S NOT WHAT YOU LOOK
AT THAT MATTERS

BUT WHAT YOU SEE.

The best among us will learn from the mistakes of the past

while the rest of us are
doomed to repeat them.

"In every
life there
comes
a day of
reckoning."

© ANDREW EVANS / PR PHOTOS

being cut off from the Grayson fortune.) Daniel isn't alone in these feelings; Charlotte is also feeling like a fish-out-of-water. Both are rejecting the Grayson way, repulsed by who their parents really are. Daniel is truly surprised and disappointed by his father's affair, and Charlotte sees through her mother's attempts to repair their relationship. Their sibling bonding at the police station solidifies their liberated stance: in the war of the Graysons, it's children versus parents.

Even in the glitzy world of *Revenge*, guilt can't be assuaged by throwing money at it; a charity endowment, a $200,000 car, or a $10-million payoff doesn't bring forgiveness or peace of mind. If guilt was so easily extinguished, both Emily and Victoria would have found happiness a long time ago.

BEST SERVED COLD Victoria knows how to dominate. Not only does she trick Lydia into doing what she wants, she then forces her into an embrace and delivers the meanest one-on-one chat ever. Do *not* threaten Queen Victoria.

WHO'S THAT GUY? If Lydia Davis is anything like the woman who plays her, Amber Valletta (b. February 9, 1974), she'll definitely have a second act. After gracing covers like *Vogue* and starring in ad campaigns for Louis Vuitton and Calvin Klein, the model transitioned to television, co-hosting MTV's fashion show, *House of Style* (1995–1996). TV and movie roles followed, including a starring turn as a do-gooding NYC socialite Allegra Cole (who is Lydia's polar opposite) in the 2005 Will Smith romantic comedy *Hitch*.

BEHIND THE SCENES *Revenge*'s drastic shift from being a takedown-of-the-week procedural to being a more traditional (but still dark) serial soap was premeditated, according to Mike Kelley. He wanted to hook viewers with a juicy premise, but, in order for *Revenge* to work for a full season (and beyond!), he felt he needed to explore the main characters and their relationships in more depth. "We wanted to give the audience some time to get know our regular characters, then build out the larger twists and turns of the story," Kelley explained to KCRW's *The Treatment*. With that accomplished in the first four episodes, "We could make it more pointed now. We could make it more personal now."

REVENGENDA What did Victoria say to Lydia to stop the speech? Is Emily astute enough to notice Nolan filming her home and to ship the Shamu cam to Lydia, but not astute enough to have noticed her own face in the New Year's Eve photo when she was packing it up? On top of the cab, Lydia blinked, which means she's not really dead, right? And if she's not, what does this mean for Emily?

REVENGESPIRATION
"Never underestimate the power of guilt, Amanda. It compels people to some pretty remarkable places." — David Clarke

REVENGE READING
HERMAN MELVILLE'S *MOBY-DICK*

The whale cam might be Nolan's way to gain better insight into who Emily is and what she's up to, but it also offers us a view of what *Revenge* is trying to accomplish. A whale is at the center of one of the greatest revenge stories in Western literature: Herman Melville's *Moby-Dick*.

First published in 1851, *Moby-Dick* follows whaling boat *Pequod*, which is led by Captain Ahab. Ahab has a singular goal in life: to hunt down and kill the great white whale that took his leg. At the time of publication, the book was a commercial failure, driving Melville to give up fiction for poetry. However, *Moby-Dick* began to gain prominence after Melville's death and it's now considered a seminal work in American literature, thanks to its sophisticated structure and timeless themes.

Captain Ahab believes that Moby-Dick represents the evil that exists in the world and that it is his obligation to destroy it. He's so driven by his singular goal that he forgets all else. He puts his crew in harm's way and manipulates them so he can continue on with his quest. (Sound familiar? Emily is constantly manipulating people to keep her plan in motion.)

However, Ahab is as much of a victim as he is an instigator. Desperate for a purposeful and meaningful life, he will not rest until he is satisfied, just like Emily. Yet Ahab's quest for revenge destroys his life just as much as it gives him purpose. Of Captain Ahab, critic M.H. Abrams wrote that he "moves us to pity because, since he is not an evil man, his misfortune is greater than he deserves; but he moves us also to fear, because we recognize similar possibilities of error in our own lesser and fallible selves." He could have just as easily been writing about Emily or Victoria. Like Ahab, their obsessions compel them to do bad things and could lead to self-destruction.

Ahab's singular vision is his ultimate downfall. He sacrifices his family, his crew, and his life to hunt down Moby-Dick. Emily does the same. She has no friends, no hobbies, and no interests beyond her revengenda. Victoria is also consumed by a singular goal: maintaining her power and status. When a threat, like Emily, arrives on the scene, she's so intent on removing it that she's willing to sacrifice something that does give her fulfillment: her son's happiness.

As an all-powerful white whale, Moby-Dick is gigantic, both figuratively and literally. The crew is never able to see his entire body at once, and the whale is only one small part of the vast ocean (a major motif in *Revenge*), a mysterious and deep place no human will ever be able to fully comprehend. Try as they might, Emily and Victoria will never be able to fully see their enemies or understand the world they inhabit. The David Clarke conspiracy goes deeper and is bigger than Emily realizes and the depths of Emily's deceit are far greater than Victoria suspects.

At the end of *Moby-Dick*, Ahab's quest fails and many lose their lives because of his obsession. As Emily further plumbs the depths of what her father and the Graysons were involved in, she needs to ask herself: how many innocent people is she willing to destroy to get what she wants?

REVENGE READING
STIEG LARSSON'S
THE GIRL WITH THE DRAGON TATTOO

Thanks to Emily's distinctive body art, Nolan christened her "the girl with the infinity tattoo." But Emily has a lot more in common with the girl with the dragon tattoo than just ink. Lisbeth Salander's creator Stieg Larsson once said, "To exact revenge for yourself or your friends is not only a right, it's an absolute duty." That sounds exactly like a quotation Emily would use in an opening narration of *Revenge*.

In Larsson's *The Girl With the Dragon Tattoo*, the first book in his Millennium Trilogy (first published in Sweden in 2005 and translated into English in 2008), Lisbeth helps disgraced journalist Mikael Blomkvist solve a decades-old murder. Lisbeth is aggressive, asocial, and deeply distrustful, thanks to an abusive childhood. When she was 12 years old, she tried to escape her father's abuse by setting him on fire. The court declared Lisbeth dangerous to herself and others, and she spent the rest of her childhood in an institution. Released at 18, she was angry at the world and often resorted to violence. She became a skilled thief, expert computer hacker, and master of disguise, who trusts only one person — Blomkvist. If you swap her dirty hoodies, black hair, and tattoos for designer clothes and a picture-perfect smile, this description easily fits Emily Thorne (although Emily had a dark hair and dirty hoodie phase of her own when she was Amanda Clarke), with tech genius Nolan Ross standing in as her partner-in-crime.

Larsson intended for Lisbeth to show how people can become disgraced by society and simply forgotten. The system failed Lisbeth, just as it failed young Amanda Clarke. In order to make peace with their past, Lisbeth and Emily take matters into their own hands, with their warped views as to what constitutes right and wrong. Lisbeth says, "There are no innocents. There are, however, different degrees of responsibility," words that could come right out of Emily's mouth. Emily's relationship with Daniel is a perfect example. He is innocent of the crimes against the Clarkes and is trying to be a better person than his parents are, but, in Emily's eyes, he's fair game because of his affiliation to those who wronged her father.

In Lisbeth's story, revenge is a complicated, emotionally exhausting, and isolating path that forever affects the avenger as much as the target. Emily seems to understand this intellectually, but will she have the strength to stay on track once things get messy?

• ● •

*"They say vengeance taken will tear the heart
and torment the conscience. If there is any truth
to it, then I now know, with certainty,
the path I'm on is the right one."*

1.06 INTRIGUE

AIRED October 26, 2011
WRITTEN BY Dan Dworkin and Jay Beattie
DIRECTED BY Tim Hunter

It's the Fourth of July, a great day for romance and revenge. Frank is on to Nolan and Emily, and Tyler is getting on Emily's nerves.

Intrigue can be both a powerful tool that helps Emily or a dangerous weapon that works against her. Emily uses intrigue to develop her persona, romance Daniel, and gain valuable information about her targets. But when she intrigues the wrong person — like Frank or Victoria — it could mean big trouble.

And that's exactly what happens in this episode. Frank is discovering Emily's secret plans, proving Nolan right — Frank is better at this than they are. In fact, Emily could learn a thing or two from him. Also an outsider, he never stops working or loses focus. Frank has become a master at keeping his emotions under wraps in order to accomplish the task at hand, while Emily is still learning how to sharpen her focus and eliminate distractions.

Frank's kept his feelings for Victoria in check for years, but now, with nothing left to lose, he lets his emotions dictate his actions. Usually the most clear-headed person in the Grayson household (he doesn't even drink, or at least doesn't drink in bars with his employer), Frank is untethered when Conrad fires him, and his passion for Victoria is no longer carefully controlled. But if we've learned anything from *Revenge*, it's that emotions get in the way, they don't guide you forward.

Take Emily's reaction to Tyler. His disruptive presence rattles her, and the always-composed Emily Thorne lets a bit more of Amanda Clarke

shine through in her impressive dressing down of Tyler at dinner. His presence may intrigue and bother her, but there's no game-playing advantage to humiliating him so publicly. Tyler seems undeterred by Emily's sniping, and calling him on his lies only distances her from Daniel and Ashley, two people she needs as allies if she wants to stay close to the Graysons.

Jack and Declan, on the other hand, only know how to be earnest. Unlike Emily and Frank, they have no ulterior motives or devious plans afoot. The Porter brothers represent the alternative. Charlotte could reject the life her parents have laid out for her and choose a happy but humble one with Declan while Emily could forgive those who wronged her and build a life with Jack, perhaps having the kind of happiness her father wanted for her.

Jack's heartfelt confession on the dock and Emily's reaction to it is a wonderfully complicated scene emotionally. Emily Thorne is supposed to be in love with Daniel, but her inner Amanda Clarke is extremely moved by Jack's loyalty and love. It seems that she more than understands the feeling Jack describes — she feels it too. Emily decides to repress her Amanda instincts (despite her declaration that "Amanda Clarke no longer exists," Amanda seems to be alive and well), to pretend not to return his affection. Her pointed opening voiceover speaks to how conflicted she is, and in response to that, she refuses to second-guess her mission. Uncertainty creates problems. Big ones.

You only have to look to the Graysons for proof of that. Conrad and Victoria use doubt to manipulate each other. Why did Frank push Lydia? Who recorded the video? What is going on with the children? As long as there are unanswered questions (and, when it comes to the Graysons, there are a ton), uncertainty keeps them together but tears them up inside.

BEST SERVED COLD Emily ruthlessly cut Tyler down at dinner, earning the "grade-A bitch" label from Ashley. Emily has zero tolerance for bullshit, and when she doesn't like someone, they better watch out.

HAMPTONS HOMAGE The episode ends with Emily saying, "The heart has reasons that reason cannot know," a quote borrowed from

17th-century philosopher Blaise Pascal's *Pensées*. This quote can be read in two ways, both applicable to *Revenge*. First, there is an incomprehensible divide between the logic of the heart and the logic of the mind. What we "should" do (intellectually) and what we want to do (emotionally) are often not the same thing, or even contradictory; witness Emily's choice to put aside her feelings for Jack to keep on her revengenda. Second, *Pensées* was written as a defense of Christianity. While Pascal was referring to the heart having faith that God exists and God has a plan, Emily is referring to her plan of revenge. Not only is she following her plan like a good disciple, she has faith that her plan will work and she is doing the right thing, no matter how off-track she feels or how many people get in the way.

BEHIND THE SCENES The scene on the dock where Jack confesses his feelings for Emily is one of Nick Wechsler's favorites in season one. "It was one of the only times I didn't hate my own performance," the ever-critical actor said. "I just found the right emotional place where I wasn't judging myself like I usually am when I'm acting. I felt good."

REVENGENDA When Frank met Conrad at the bar, Frank insinuated that they both are involved in things more sinister than covering up Conrad's extramarital affairs. What did they do? Daniel may be cut off, but he still lives by the philosophy that money can solve most problems (as he demonstrates by paying off the lobster toughs). Will he run out of dough before he realizes this isn't the case? How far will Tyler go to get what he wants? What *does* he want?

REVENGESPIRATION
"I'm rich. You're not. Who cares?" — Charlotte to Declan

"Within each of us is the capacity for both good and evil. But those of us who are able to blur the moral dividing line hold the true power."

1.07 CHARADE

AIRED November 2, 2011
WRITTEN BY Mark B. Perry and Joe Fazzio
DIRECTED BY Sanford Bookstaver

It's Conrad and Victoria's 25th wedding anniversary. Instead of a celebration, it's chaos.

Emily's poignant voiceover at the beginning of the episode quotes *Hamlet*: "God has given you one face, and you make yourself another." This sentiment is true for most of the characters on the show — it feels like everyone has built an identity on lies and misdirection — but it's also true for *Revenge* as a series. It began as a procedural, with Emily knocking off one victim per episode. But with its recent episodes, *Revenge* has changed its face. Now the show is about the big picture: the David Clarke conspiracy, what it takes to make it in the Hamptons, and the choices people make to build and maintain their public personas.

Maintaining this face might be the biggest challenge of all. Victoria is clearly fed up with the charade she and Conrad have been putting on for 25 years. As she sees those she loves get hurt because of the choices she's made — David Clarke, her children, and, to a lesser extent, her former friend Lydia and former security guard, Frank — she questions whether the charade is worth it. Conrad, on the other hand, seems completely fine with it. His only regret is that Victoria never loved him the way he wanted her to, and he is willing to fill that void with Lydia as long as the family's public image is maintained. But Lydia also offers Conrad an example to follow. If Lydia gets a chance to start over after a nasty divorce, a public shaming, a physical attack, and a five-story fall off the roof of her building, Conrad can surely survive a marriage based on lies and convenience for a second chance of his own.

Another couple bonding over lies is the ambitious duo of Tyler and Ashley. Since Ashley's friendship with Emily isn't doing her any favors in the social status department, she's become increasingly reliant on Tyler's favor with the Graysons to open doors for her. Tyler didn't have to tell her the truth about his own situation, but doing so actually works to his advantage. Ashley can help him achieve his endgame, especially since she was so receptive to his plans, and now he'll have company executing his con, usually a lonely business. It's far better to have someone there beside you, to share the experience. It's why Conrad and Victoria have stuck it out for so long, and why Emily is leaning on Nolan as an ally in her quest.

Nolan is also running a charade. In public, he's an awkward doofus. But at home, he's a confident man. His demeanor is different in the two spheres of his life, his clothes are different, and even his drink of choice is different. (He drinks scotch at home, not his beloved Malibu Bay Breeze.) He tried to record Emily in her home in "Guilt" to gather information; here he records his and Tyler's special time together, but it's unclear why. He's undoubtedly loyal to the Clarkes, but, like most everyone else, he has a few cards left up his sleeve.

Frank Stevens, on the other hand, is out of cards. (He didn't blink when he was lying in the bushes, so it's safe to assume he's actually dead.) But with his exit comes the entrance of a new intriguing player: the real Emily Thorne, who works as a stripper on the seedy side of an upstate town. Her Amanda Clarke charade is the most interesting of all, because there's no obvious gain from pretending to be the daughter of a reviled man. As far as we know, there's no one she wants to hurt, no one she wants to con, and no money she's after. But by embracing her new identity, hers is biggest charade of all: she doesn't have to pretend to be someone she's not. She actually gets to *be* someone she's not.

BEST SERVED COLD The real Emily Thorne is a badass. She keeps her cool during Frank's interrogation and then calmly takes a tire iron to his brain. She didn't need to kill Frank — she probably has a lot less to lose than the fake Emily Thorne if the truth is exposed — but she did it to protect fake Emily. Oh, and because she's a little off her rocker.

HAMPTONS HOMAGE Nolan claims he's a "3" on the Kinsey scale, a metric of sexual orientation determined by Alfred Kinsey and Wardell Pomeroy in 1948 in their influential publication *Sexual Behaviour in the Human Male*. Being a "3" allows Nolan to be who he wants to be when he wants to be it, able to manipulate others with his sexuality as he sees fit. Fitting, considering the theme of the episode.

The Allenwood Federal Correctional Complex really exists. It's located in Union County, Pennsylvania, and currently houses 2,900 inmates. The Allenwood Juvenile Detention Center, as it's called on *Revenge*, is a fictional re-imagining of this famed prison with two big changes: the real Allenwood doesn't house minors or women.

WHO'S THAT GUY? Carol Christine Hilaria Pounder — a.k.a. C.C.H. Pounder — plays Emily's warden and protector, Sharon Stiles. Pounder has worked consistently in film, television, and voice work since 1979. Her most notable roles include Dr. Angela Hicks on *ER* (1994–1997), an Emmy-nominated performance as Detective Claudette Wyms on *The Shield* (2002–2008), and Na'vi spiritual leader Mo'at in *Avatar* (2009), which just happens to be the highest-grossing film of all time.

BORROWED FROM THE BOOK Dantès escapes prison by swapping places with another prisoner. Emily escapes the prison of being Amanda Clarke by swapping identities with Emily Thorne. Neither of these plans unfolds as anticipated: Dantès is tossed out to sea to sink to a watery grave, and Emily must now constantly deal with the ocean that is Fauxmanda's neediness.

BEHIND THE SCENES If you thought the hook-up between Tyler and Nolan was steamy, you should have seen what was left on the editing room floor. "We really went for it, Gabe and I, and then it didn't air," Holmes told *After Elton*. Holmes thinks ABC made the final decision about the scene's cuts, but Mike Kelley said the decision was simply an editorial one. "The kiss wasn't, for me, as interesting as the intention," he said. "I just thought, 'Let's hold off and let's make the scene look beautiful.'"

When Emily and Daniel are frolicking on the beach, you can see a tattoo on Daniel's right ribcage. Unlike Emily's infinity tattoo, Daniel's tattoo is real. It's Latin for "Don't let the fuckers get you down," Bowman revealed to Ellen DeGeneres. "There was a time in my life I was a bit rebellious and I was like, 'Don't let them get you down, Josh!' and I just planted it right on the side of my ribs." It's a message that also resonates for Daniel, which is probably why the *Revenge* team didn't cover it up.

REVENGENDA Why is the warden offering revenge advice to Emily and so keen to protect her from Frank's snooping? How did fake Emily manipulate real Emily into exchanging identities with her? What are Nolan's plans for his sex tape? And is he really a "3" on the Kinsey, or was he just playing Tyler?

REVENGESPIRATION
"Never underestimate your enemy." — Emily Thorne
"And never let your guard down." — Warden Sharon Stiles

REVENGE READING
WILLIAM SHAKESPEARE'S *HAMLET*

Shakespeare's *Hamlet* is a story about deceit, indecisiveness, and revenge. When Hamlet returns home to Denmark for his father's funeral, he is shocked to discover that his mother is already remarried to his uncle Claudius, the new king. He's even more shocked when his father's ghost appears and tells him that Claudius murdered him in order to take the throne. Hamlet spends the bulk of the play debating whether or not he should avenge his father's murder by killing Claudius.

Hamlet can't decide what to do because his knowledge about what happened is built on a set of assumptions. His ghostly father tells him Claudius is a murderer (not unlike how Emily's dead father speaks to her through his journals), but no physical evidence of the crime exists. To figure it out, Hamlet lurks around Claudius and his inner circle acting mad, just as Emily works her way into the Hamptons elite by acting harmless. Others don't see the mad prince or the sweet girl next door as threatening. Hamlet and Emily use this false sense of security to gain intel and the upper hand on their enemies.

Separating the truth from the charade is difficult for Hamlet, in part because Claudius is such a dynamic, manipulative speaker, and he uses this skill to strengthen his rule. Victoria, in many ways, is like Claudius. She says one thing but means entirely another. Claudius is obsessed with maintaining his power over Denmark, just as Victoria is with her domain in the Hamptons. Neither one rules justly, and for Emily and Hamlet, these subsequent destructive actions further strengthen their resolves to exact revenge.

Even if their actions are justified, that doesn't mean the story will end prettily. After Hamlet finally makes a decision, he (spoiler!) murders Claudius in a messy battle wherein Hamlet watches his mother die before dying himself. No one escapes the havoc Hamlet's revenge plan has wrought. Everyone loses (except Fortinbras) and it's difficult to say if Hamlet's plan to avenge his father's murder was worth it all in the end.

Emily is familiar with *Hamlet* — she quotes the play in her opening narration — but either she's certain that her fate will differ from Hamlet's or she's okay with facing her end as long as her opponents suffer alongside her.

"There's an old saying about those who cannot remember the past being condemned to repeat it.
But those of us who refuse to forget the past are condemned to relive it."

1.08 TREACHERY

AIRED November 16, 2011
WRITTEN BY Ryan Scott
DIRECTED BY Bobby Roth

The presence of the real Emily Thorne causes big problems for the fake Emily Thorne. The death of Frank solves some problems, but creates a few more.

  Revenge served up two big twists in "Treachery" — Lydia has amnesia and a mysterious new girl has come to town — that present Victoria and Emily with unforeseen obstacles to overcome in order to keep their plans in motion.

  These twists are part of a storytelling strategy that *Revenge* does so very well: breathing new life into tired soap tropes. Switched identities, miraculous survivals, and conveniently timed amnesia are all staple storylines for the soaps, in both daytime and primetime. But they work here for three reasons. First, they are played straight. There are no winks to the audience that *Revenge* knows they are entering well-worn and campy territory. They go there and they own it. Second, these soapy storylines zip by and are never the focus of any given episode. Instead, the characters' emotions and interactions stay center stage. Third, they help balance the show's darker themes and elements. These people are nasty and do terrible, terrible things. By contrasting that with storylines too ridiculous to be believable, *Revenge* creates a frothy and frightening fantasy world that allows viewers to sit back and enjoy. *Revenge* never loses its focus or its sense of fun, even as the soap storylines get dialed up to almost ridiculous extremes as the season goes on — which is part of what makes it such a successful show.

  The real Emily Thorne (henceforth referred to as Fauxmanda for the sake of clarity. Thanks, Nolan!) is a girl who has been used, abused, disappointed, and let down time and time again. This is a girl who's had to stand up for herself from a very young age, who no one — not even the warden whose job it is to watch over her — believed in. It's no wonder she became so attached to Amanda Clarke. Amanda was the first person who ever helped her out and became invested in her. Fauxmanda sees in Emily a soul mate and sister: someone else who the world rejected, then kicked when they were down. Fauxmanda's connection to Emily is the only thing she has. (Since she blew through $500,000 in a handful of years.) She has no idea that she's just a pawn in Emily's game. This defining connection propels Fauxmanda to stay in the Hamptons, despite a free plane ticket to anywhere in the world and the promise of a new identity. The allure of Jack Porter helps too. A relationship with Jack gives Fauxmanda the purpose she's been looking for and strengthens the bond she shares with Emily.

While Emily is trying to keep her past a secret, Victoria is attempting to rewrite hers. Lydia's convenient amnesia gives Victoria the opportunity for damage-control. As her marriage deteriorates, Victoria is isolated, lonely without her former go-to allies Conrad and Frank. Forcing Lydia back under her control (and under her roof) works to Victoria's advantage on multiple levels. Guilt is a powerful motivator for Victoria, and Lydia's predicament is no exception. Choosing to take care of Lydia lets Victoria work through her guilt. But it's also self-serving. Under her watchful care, Victoria can monitor Lydia, direct her memories by reinforcing their friendship, drive a wedge between Lydia and Conrad, and protect the Grayson reputation.

Emily has learned the power of divulging and controlling information about her past. By revealing she went to Allenwood, she manages to protect her reputation with Daniel. The revelation serves her revengenda: it proves she's fallible and it gives Daniel the impression she is opening up to him, now more willing to be her "true self" around him. Like Victoria with Lydia, Emily carefully and purposefully shapes Daniel's perception of her.

As *Revenge* progresses, the similarities between Emily and Victoria are more apparently showcased. Both are defined by the past and doing everything they can to shape their future. The difference lies in how they've gotten to this point. Emily was a victim of others' actions, her fate thrust upon her, whereas Victoria chose her path. But now that Emily is in control, if she continues down this road to vengeance, she may end up just like Victoria: with everything she ever wanted, but no one to share it with.

BEST SERVED COLD Lydia doesn't even remember Emily, but Emily is quick with a double-edged comment about Lydia's health and beach house, anyway. Way to kick a girl when she's down, Ems.

HAMPTONS HOMAGE When real Emily arrives at Nolan's home, he welcomes her by asking if she's a fan of *Gears of War 3*, a video game series that follows a former military soldier who is unable to save his father in battle and is eventually sentenced to prison because of his father's crimes — not unlike Amanda Clarke.

The drink Fauxmanda makes for Jack, the Black Dahlia, can be made with 3.5 ounces citrus vodka, 3/4 ounces raspberry liqueur, and 3/4 ounces Kahlua coffee liqueur. Add ice and shake. The Black Dahlia has more significance for *Revenge* than introducing its viewers to a delicious drink. It's also the nickname of the most notorious murders in Hollywood history. Elizabeth Short was an aimless drifter (like Fauxmanda), whose story began with an unsolved murder (like *Revenge*). As a young girl, her father disappeared and was thought to be dead (not unlike David Clarke), before being found alive across the country. (Hmmm . . .) After Elizabeth was brutally and bizarrely murdered, she developed an unwarranted reputation in the media (like David Clarke). Her murder was never solved, and it came to define her surviving family members (like Emily).

BEHIND THE SCENES Watch Nolan when he encounters something new or is given a drink. He will smell it. He smells everything: sawdust, crossanwiches, and whisky are all subjected to Nolan's nose. It was a quirk Gabriel Mann gave Nolan early on, and it stuck. Mike Kelley loved it: "I think it's hilarious." Emily VanCamp agreed and loves what Mann brings to the show. "Gabriel took that character and made it his own," she said to the *Sydney Morning Herald.* "He took a risk, really. He's very funny but unbelievably professional. He brings comic relief to the show, and god knows we need that."

REVENGENDA How will Emily keep up on her revenge plotting with Daniel shacking up with her? What will Victoria do once Lydia gets her memory back? How will Emily deal with Fauxmanda's choice to stick around the Hamptons? Why *did* Jack take romantic advice from Nolan, anyway?

REVENGESPIRATION
"Violence is a short-sighted solution when it really comes to handling your enemies. There are better ways to go about it. Smarter ways." — Warden Sharon Stiles

REVENGE READING
PATRICIA HIGHSMITH'S
THE TALENTED MR. RIPLEY

In Patricia Highsmith's 1955 psychological thriller, Tom Ripley, a small-time con artist posing as a recent Princeton graduate, is sent to Italy to convince Dickie Greenleaf, the son of wealthy parents, to give up his pedestrian life as an aspiring artist to come home. What happens instead is that Ripley cons his way into Dickie's life, manipulates his friends, drives a wedge between Dickie and his not-quite-girlfriend Marge (who sees right through Tom and hates him from the very beginning), wears Dickie's clothes and adopts his mannerisms. Dickie and Tom's relationship is extraordinarily intense, bordering on sexual. When Dickie is bored with Tom (their friendship is based on a mutual understanding: Tom gains access to Dickie's privileged lifestyle, but he must constantly entertain Dickie), Tom becomes increasingly frustrated, angry, and desperate. He views the economic and cultural divide between them as unfair and believes it can only be closed if he kills Dickie and takes over his life.

Tyler hasn't plotted Daniel's murder, but he gets away with almost everything else, from posing as a student and wearing Daniel's clothing to convincing the Graysons that he, and only he, can convince Daniel that his own pedestrian life choice, tending bar, is not worth the sacrifice of his family name and legacy.

Both Tom and Tyler desperately want to be someone; they see the world as fundamentally unjust and can't discern why Dickie and Daniel have the world at their feet and they don't. Of Tom, Highsmith writes, "He loved possessions, not masses of them, but a select few that he did not part with. They gave a man self-respect. Not ostentation but quality, and the love that cherished the quality. Possessions reminded him that he existed, and made him enjoy his existence." The same could be said of Tyler. He's constantly mentioning his family's wealth and property Possessions, in the eyes of Tom and Tyler, tell the world that you matter, that you have status, and it's only because Dickie and Daniel have plenty of possessions and plenty of means to acquire more that they can turn their backs on wealth and yearn for simpler lifestyles. It's a choice only the privileged could make, and it pisses off Tom and Tyler.

Tom doesn't just offer insight into Tyler. He also offers insight into Fauxmanda. Like Tom, Fauxmanda is trying to take over Emily's life by assuming her characteristics and old identity. While she doesn't want the material possessions and social status that come with Emily's wealth as much as Tyler wants Jack's, she manipulates the situation to get what she thinks she deserves: a place to belong and someone to love.

Ripley also sheds light on Emily. Written from Tom's perspective, its insight into his mind and his reasoning allows readers to feel empathy and understanding toward a character who could, from a distance, be seen as simply evil and without a conscience. *Revenge* uses this same narrative technique in telling the story of Emily Thorne. She's coldly and methodologically destroying lives. Sometimes those people are innocent (or, at least, lesser degrees of guilty). But because we're allowed to see inside her mind, and understand her rationale, we side with her, understand her, and cheer for her.

● ● ●

"The most dangerous secrets a person can bury are those we keep from ourselves."

1.09 SUSPICION

AIRED November 23, 2011
WRITTEN BY Salvatore Stabile
DIRECTED BY Bethany Rooney

When Emily can't get rid of Fauxmanda as easily as she thought, she turns to her revenge sensei for help.

Emily has two big thorns in her side: Tyler and Fauxmanda. Not only are they setting up roadblocks on her road to revenge, their presence increases the possibility of people noticing Emily may not be who she says see is: one knows the truth and the other is on to it. Bringing in Takeda helps Emily deal with them, but it also has the added benefit of giving Emily the opportunity to re-focus and re-assess why she's in the Hamptons in the first place.

Tyler is a reminder to Emily about how far she's come since leaving juvie nearly 10 years ago, but he also reminds her how fragile her façade is. Anyone with the slightest suspicious inkling could catch on to her, and it's in her best interest to eliminate such people before they become problems. While Tyler is very much part of Emily's present, digging into her past, Fauxmanda is part of Emily's past, clawing her way into the future. As reckless and emotional as Fauxmanda may be, she represents the one real relationship Emily has had in her life since her father was taken away. If Emily moves forward with her plan, it means she'll not only have to turn her back on her childhood sweetheart and teenage best friend, but destroy the only real relationship she's had since her father was framed.

Emily's beef with Tyler and her need to keep Fauxmanda out of the way is causing all sorts of problems with Daniel, Ashley, and Jack — people who don't deserve mistreatment. This is very much a turning point for Emily: does she move past this and do what Takeda wants? Or does she try her best to keep the relationships around her intact but possibly raise more suspicion in the process?

Tyler has the clothes (thanks to Daniel's closet and Nolan's credit card) and the ambition to make it in the Hamptons. He proved that at the investors' party with his graceful schmoozing and willingness to do *anything* to score an investor and beat Daniel in Conrad's little competition. He tries to turn every moment, even one as casual as a company volleyball tournament, into an opportunity to leverage. Money (or a reasonable facsimile of wealth) may open doors, but becoming a viable, integral part of Hamptons society takes craft, polish, and skill — attributes both Tyler and Emily had to learn.

Whereas Tyler and Emily create opportunities to weasel their way into Hamptons society, Fauxmanda takes advantage of the one that was handed to her, Amanda Clarke's identity. She has no qualms about dressing or speaking the right way, because she has something Tyler doesn't have: a name. Simply by virtue of calling herself Amanda

Clarke, she knows she has a place in the Hamptons, however controversial. Fauxmanda realizes that her adopted name will open doors — or in Jack's case, his heart. The same is true for Daniel. His name opens doors for him: it's okay if he bumbles his way through an investor meeting because he is a Grayson.

But names aren't everything. Just ask Victoria. Her name ensures her position but it doesn't guarantee her allies. That's why she made a truce with Emily and even invited Ashley to brunch. Five episodes ago, there's no way Victoria would have entertained Ashley socially or let her call her Victoria. She's desperate for a way inside Emily's mind, and an ambitious social climber who understands the value of the Grayson name just might do. For now.

BEST SERVED COLD Both Madeleine Stowe and Emily VanCamp deserve applause for their performances when Victoria comes over to Emily's beach house to make a peace offering. There are so many layers to their words, their agendas, and the false show they put on for each other as the two mask their mutual hatred, grief, and disappointment in how their plans are unfolding. Despite the sparse dialogue, this heavy stuff came across simply and beautifully.

HAMPTONS HOMAGE This episode kicks off with Emily borrowing a quote from legendary screenwriter Ben Hecht: "A lover is apt to be as full of secrets from himself as is the object of his love from him." Hecht is one of the most successful Hollywood screenwriters of all time, penning or working on classic films such as *Scarface, Some Like It Hot, Gone With the Wind, Wuthering Heights,* and *His Girl Friday. Special bonus trivia:* Hecht's 1934 film *Viva Villa!* is the story of Mexican revolutionary general Pancho Villa, who seeks revenge for the murder of his father by killing the executioner responsible for his death.

BORROWED FROM THE BOOK Dantès had a "revenge sensei" of his own in Abbé Faria, a fellow prisoner Dantès befriends. During their many years imprisoned together, Faria teaches Dantès about history, art, culture, and how to fight. Dantès would never have had the knowledge or the know-how to become the Count had it not been for Faria. While Emily had a few assistants along the way, it's safe to assume she learned martial arts, Japanese, the art of revenge, and who knows what else from Takeda.

BEHIND THE SCENES If you enjoy Emily's revenge sensei, you have the ABC international sales team to thank for his existence. Japan was keen on airing *Revenge* in primetime (a rare occurrence for an American show) and ABC felt that a Japanese character could seal the deal. Kelley and his writing team didn't mind, as they were playing with the idea of bringing a "revenge mentor" for Emily on board anyway and created Satoshi Takeda. "They just came both at the perfect time," Kelley said.

REVENGENDA Where did Conrad take Lydia? What are Nolan's plans for Tyler — and Tyler's plans for Nolan? With Tyler and Fauxmanda causing more problems than ever, what will Emily Thorne do now?

REVENGESPIRATION
"Remember: inside the viper's nest, you must be a viper too." — Satoshi Takeda

REVENGE READING
MARY SHELLEY'S *FRANKENSTEIN*

When Emily says that making money is in Daniel's DNA, he says his family's ability to generate wealth is "like mad science to the Frankensteins." It turns out that money making and monster making have quite a bit in common: both change the perspective of the world for the maker and both have scary unintended consequences.

Originally published in 1818, *Frankenstein; or, The Modern Prometheus* is considered to be the first science fiction novel. Victor Frankenstein, obsessed with understanding the secret of life, builds a creature of his own. When the creature ends up being completely hideous, Frankenstein runs away in horror. Just as fear causes Frankenstein to flee, fear propelled the Graysons to frame David Clarke, creating their own monster, the fictitious David Clarke the Terrorist.

When Frankenstein abandons his creation, the monster ends up alone in a world he is unprepared for. The monster adapts by discovering a family in the woods. He teaches himself language and culture by listening to their conversations and reading their discarded books, which is mimicked on *Revenge* in how Emily infiltrates the Hamptons. She spends years not only training and studying to be physically prepared for her quest, she also studies to be socially and culturally prepared. Her entire "Emily Thorne" persona is an act — which is partly why her presence makes Victoria so uneasy.

Both Frankenstein and Victoria struggle with what their desires brought into the world, and realize that they should have accepted not only their limits of knowledge and power, but also the consequences of their actions. Their creations show the worst they have inside themselves: their greed, ambition, selfishness, and need for power. With this new perspective, Victor and Victoria better understand how they made the world a worse place. Guilt and shame are powerful motivators, even more so than greed and ambition. Victor's guilt becomes so overwhelming that he chooses to absolve himself and confess his sins before he dies. As guilt continues to eat away at Victoria, will she succumb to the same fate?

● ● ●

"Always question where your loyalties lie. The people you trust will expect it, your greatest enemies will desire it, and those you treasure the most will, without fail, abuse it."

1.10 LOYALTY

AIRED December 7, 2011
WRITTEN BY Wendy Calhoun and Nikki Toscano
DIRECTED BY J. Miller Tobin

Emily betrays Nolan in an effort to stop Tyler, but encourages Fauxmanda to cozy up to Jack. Takeda questions her ability to finish what she started, and the Grayson divorce begins.

Well, Takeda's presence certainly got under Emily's skin this week. She is a jerk to her most loyal friend-in-revenge, Nolan, and does a complete 180 on Fauxmanda, going from wanting her halfway around the world to encouraging her relationship with Jack. The theme of the week was loyalty, but this episode left viewers — and Takeda — questioning where Emily's loyalties lie.

There's no question that Nolan is unfailingly loyal to Emily, helping her, protecting her identity, and feeding her essential information about the Graysons and her father. Yet Emily never seems to appreciate his loyalty. Instead, she's always testing him and challenging his ability to be Robin to her Batman. Can he Photoshop this photo? Will he encrypt this video? Will he invest with Tyler? No, wait, can he pull those funds instead? His relationship with Emily is give-give-give, and he's tiring of being taken for granted. Tyler may be using him, but that relationship has an above-board give-and-take. (That is, until Tyler goes off his meds and throws Nolan's computer in a pool. Not cool.) Nolan expects the same courtesy from Emily; instead, she throws him under the bus. Her loyalties lie with her plan, nowhere else.

Takeda believes otherwise. He believes her focus is clouded because she's in love with Daniel. While she denies it, it's easy to understand his perspective. Does she really need to encourage Daniel to patch things up with his mother and pursue a career at Grayson Global? Given how much Victoria relies on her children to feel a sense of purpose and self-worth, you would think that Emily would encourage the opposite approach and do everything she can to isolate Daniel from Victoria. But maybe, underneath it all, she understands the importance of parental relationships. She looks completely devastated when Nolan says her father would be disappointed in her. And her entire plan — her entire purpose — exists because of an undying loyalty to her father. Maybe she thinks she can take down Victoria without destroying Daniel's relationship with her.

It's unclear whether Emily is protecting Daniel or setting him up for an even bigger fall, and this same ambiguity exists in her treatment of Jack. From the beginning, she wanted to keep Jack out of the crossfire. But here she is, pushing Fauxmanda closer to him, letting him believe that his childhood friend came back for him and Sammy. Emily isn't going to keep Fauxmanda around forever, so is she setting up Jack to be crushed?

Emily knows to always question where her loyalties lie. But is she also questioning where her heart is?

BEST SERVED COLD Emily goes behind Nolan's back and uses information about his relationship with Tyler to take Tyler down. She's willing to do anything to get what she wants — even potentially destroy the relationship with her tech support and friend.

HAMPTONS HOMAGE Nolan refers to Fauxmanda as Emily's "secret sharer" (see page 146) and "single white female" in the same breath. "Single white female" refers to the 1990 John Lutz book (*SWF Seeks Same*) and the 1992 film adaptation (*Single White Female*) about a girl whose roommate seems like a perfect match. Until the roommate begins to copy everything the girl does and reveals a manipulative, dangerous, and controlling side — not unlike Tom Ripley in *The Talented Mr. Ripley*. The film had immense influence in popular culture, with the "single white female" becoming a popular film and TV trope.

WHO'S THAT GUY? James McCaffrey (Ryan Huntley) is best known for playing a dead man. On *Rescue Me* (2004–2011) he played Jimmy Keefe, a firefighter who perished in 9/11 and whose ghost both torments and acts a moral compass for his cousin, Tommy Gavin. McCaffrey's other notable role isn't on film at all: he's the narrator of the popular videogame series *Max Payne*.

BORROWED FROM THE BOOK Charlotte and Declan's relationship is based on Maximilian Morrel and his love for Valentine de Villefort, the daughter of the prosecutor who helped convict Dantès. Valentine has a father who ignores her and a stepmother who can't stand her. She is supposed to marry someone of equal social and financial standing, not fall for the poor son of a ship owner. Despite their challenges, Valentine and Maximilian declare their love for each other and vow to stay together, no matter what.

BEHIND THE SCENES Emily Thorne may be fluent in Japanese, but Emily VanCamp can't speak a word of the language. Even though she had her lines memorized, she discreetly taped them to Sanada's clothing during their training sequence, just in case.

REVENGENDA Is lawyer Ryan Huntley Emily's next target, or is he working for her? Will Emily be able to fix her relationship with Nolan? How much crazier will Tyler get without his medication? How ugly will the Grayson divorce become? Now that Victoria knows Amanda Clarke is back in town, what does she plan to do?

REVENGESPIRATION
"If you let your emotions guide you, you will fail." — Satoshi Takeda

REVENGE READING
JOSEPH CONRAD'S "THE SECRET SHARER"

Nolan refers to Fauxmanda as Emily's "secret sharer," and this seemingly off-hand comment sheds light on Mike Kelley's inspiration behind Emily and Fauxmanda's relationship: "The Secret Sharer" by Joseph Conrad. This short story, originally published in *Harper's Magazine* in 1910, is about an unnamed insecure captain of a new ship who takes aboard a stranger he discovers swimming in the ocean. The stranger is fleeing after accidentally killing a fellow sailor. The captain hides this stranger away from his crew, and they share a very intense, possessive relationship; the captain often refers to the stranger as his "second self" or "double." As the stranger toys with the captain, the captain becomes more confident, cunning, and manipulative, inspiring a complicated, psychosexual power struggle between the two men.

The similarities between the captain and the stranger and Emily and Fauxmanda are striking. A murder brings each pair together and the characters involved become completely intertwined and dependent on each other. Both relationships are extremely co-dependent and intense. The captain and the stranger feed off each other, bringing out the very best and very worst in each other, just as Emily and Fauxmanda balance each other's extremes. Emily could afford to be a little more carefree, whereas Fauxmanda could afford to be a little more cautious.

Ultimately, while both relationships are intensely loyal, they exist primarily out of mutual convenience. The captain wants control of his ship, the stranger wants to escape persecution for his crime, Emily wants Victoria off her back, and Fauxmanda wants a place to call home. And they all get what they want — eventually.

"Duress impacts relationships in one of two ways: it either tears people apart or strengthens their connection, binding them tightly in a common objective."

1.11 DURESS

AIRED January 4, 2012
WRITTEN BY Elle Triedman
DIRECTED BY Jamie Babbit

Daniel gets an unwelcome birthday surprise when an unmedicated Tyler shows up to the party with a gun and isn't afraid to use it.

Tyler's presence in the Hamptons has been building toward a big showdown and "Duress" delivers it. A gun pointed at Emily's head reminds viewers that she is playing a very dangerous game — and it might not end until her blood is on the floor.

Tyler struggled to be accepted in the Hamptons, to establish himself as a player in the Grayson world, and in this final breakdown, we finally understand why. He can no longer take the pressure: his family abandoned him in his hour of need and he was left to deal with his illness solo. All it takes to get the unhinged Tyler to hit pause on his killing spree is his brother, offering an apology for the past and a promise to help in the future. The potential to belong is more enticing for Tyler than that of payback. Danny Boy has it all: looks, money, a bright future, a pretty girl who loves him, and a family who worships the ground he walks on. Tyler has none of that. As satisfying as revenge would have been, a true connection with someone is the ultimate prize. It's why Charlotte is drawn to Declan, and Daniel to Emily; why Victoria and Conrad are so determined to maintain ties to their children; and why the Porter brothers always stick together.

Emily, slowly but surely, is learning this lesson. Her relationship with Nolan is the only honest one she has. It grounds her and keeps her from spinning off into Tyler-like crazytown territory. As events move outside Emily's control, it's up to Nolan to prevent her from making rash decisions that could compromise her end goal.

Victoria's own goal (currently) is winning in the Grayson divorce. We learn that their relationship has been a lie since the beginning: she pretended to be pregnant to con him into marrying her. Victoria has been manipulating people long before she became the queen of the Hamptons and long before she betrayed David Clarke. Her entire life is built on lies and deception, which is why she works so hard in the present to prevent the past from being exposed. At her core, Victoria is simply a con artist creating an elaborate illusion, like Tyler — only she's more successful at keeping up the ruse. When the pressure is on, Tyler cracked, but Victoria carries on.

Which is exactly how Emily reacts. She applies pressure right back: calling Tyler on his crap, meddling in the Grayson divorce proceedings, and amping up her relationship with Daniel. Emily's presence puts pressure on Victoria's relationship with Daniel, her beloved son and her one unbreakable tie to the Grayson fortune, and Emily reminds Victoria that she will never truly feel at ease — since her empire is built on a foundation of fakery. Emily's suggestion of a clambake for Daniel's birthday shows she doesn't need to put on airs or stage elaborate parties to remind everyone of her importance and means. Emily's effortlessness and wealth are constant reminders to Victoria that her own life is one big illusion, and the curtain could rise at any moment. And when the curtain rises, will Victoria respond like Emily and take advantage of the situation? Or will she pull a Tyler and completely unravel?

BEST SERVED COLD Ashton Holmes is the MVP of this episode. His performance as a rapidly unraveling Tyler is a delight to watch, equally over-the-top and wonderfully subtle. He calls Conrad "Connie"! And in case you didn't realize his soul is broken, he stares into a broken mirror! He sweats like crazy when he threatens Emily! As his mind unravels, his wardrobe follows! He stabs Nolan! Even though Tyler is totally crazy and a threat to Emily's game plan, it is almost disappointing to see him go. Almost.

HAMPTONS HOMAGE When Nolan learns that Tyler's brother is coming, he notes that the Hamptons "could always use another sexy surgeon," a gentle jibe at another Hamptons-set television show, USA Network's *Royal Pains*, which follows a group of doctors who run a private on-call medical practice for their wealthy patients.

WHO'S THAT GUY? The casting of Merrin Dungey (Conrad's lawyer Barbara Snow) is a nod to that *other* show about a young woman trying to right the wrong in the world by using covert means, multiple identities, and sneaky schemes: *Alias*. Dungey played Sydney Bristrow's best friend Francie Calfo (2001–2006). Dungey's other TV work includes playing Malcolm's teacher on *Malcolm in the Middle* (2000–2004) and Kelly Palmer on *The King of Queens* (1999–2007).

BORROWED FROM THE BOOK Albert, Mercédès and Fernand's son, decides to honor the Count's arrival with a lavish breakfast. Maximilian Morrel (in this case Dantès' Jack Porter) arrives as a guest of a man whose life he saved. No one appreciates his presence, just as the Graysons are frustrated with the presence of Jack, Declan, and Fauxmanda at Daniel's lavish birthday party. This party is the first time Dantès encounters the son of Monsieur Morrel. He complicates Dantès' revenge plans, as Dantès questions his actions and motivations and must decide if the possibility of hurting the one family who was good to him is worth hurting those he feels deserve punishment, a quandary Emily knows too well.

BEHIND THE SCENES If you watch Emily Thorne closely, you'll notice she doesn't move, even when she's being held at gunpoint. She doesn't fidget, she doesn't blink, and she doesn't play with her hair. She is, as Nolan points out, in control at every moment. This lack of motion was the brainchild of Phillip Noyce, who encouraged Emily VanCamp to be

still during her scenes. VanCamp said this direction really helped her get in the mindset of her character. "With the girl-next-door characters I have played, I wasn't really conscious of their movements. They moved differently, and there's something strange about Emily," she said to *TV Line*. "Emily is almost robotic. She's numb."

REVENGENDA There's no way Tyler is gone for good, is there? He knows about Emily's floorboards! Will Fauxmanda start digging into David Clarke's past? How much dirtier can the Grayson divorce get? Was Nolan putting the moves on Ashley? Where did Big Ed, Nolan's bodyguard, go?

REVENGESPIRATION
"Blackmail. It isn't just for breakfast anymore." — Nolan Ross

REVENGE READING
ROBERT LOUIS STEVENSON'S
STRANGE CASE OF DR. JEKYLL AND MR. HYDE

Emily may have called Tyler "Dr. Jekyll and Mr. Hyde," but she could have said that about pretty much any character on *Revenge*, including herself.

Strange Case of Dr. Jekyll and Mr. Hyde, an 1886 novella by Robert Louis Stevenson, has gained pop culture prominence thanks to over 100 film, radio, and stage adaptations. Dr. Jekyll is a respected physician who unleashes his dark side through a potion, which turns him into the evil Edward Hyde. As the story progresses, Jekyll loses control over Hyde; eventually Hyde becomes the dominant personality. The story of Jekyll and Hyde is now closely associated with "split personalities" and the inner battle between good and evil, but Stevenson's original story was more complex than that. So are the "split personalities" found on *Revenge*.

Jekyll, like Emily, has a perfect public image. He's a wealthy doctor and noted philanthropist with an impeccable home. However, he's not as innocent or moral as he seems. Jekyll wants an outlet for his inner darkness and is initially delighted to have Hyde. Jekyll can sit back and enjoy his mischief, just Emily enjoys her early takedowns. Being bad is just a game. But as Jekyll loses control of Hyde and he causes greater destruction, Jekyll begins to understand the ramifications of what he's done, just as Emily begins to understand the unforeseen consequences of unleashing her revenge plan. Each attack has a ripple effect in their respective communities, innocent people get hurt, and it becomes increasingly difficult to control the outcome.

Jekyll claims "man is not truly one, but truly two"; everyone has a good side and a bad side. Jekyll and Emily aren't the only ones. Victoria hides a ruthless fighter and a passionate woman underneath her icy exterior. Daniel hides an emotional wild child underneath his all-American do-gooder persona. Conrad hides a scheming moneymaker underneath a good businessman and family man. Ashley hides an ambitious social climber underneath a perky party-planner personality. And Tyler hides a social-climbing sociopath underneath his Harvard boy exterior.

At the end of *Strange Case of Dr. Jekyll and Mr. Hyde*, evil reigns over the good doctor. Hyde consumes Jekyll, and the consequences of what he's done will never be completely known or understood. Will Emily suffer the same regrets as Dr. Jekyll?

• ● •

"Some words are immortal. Long-buried or even burned, they're destined to be reborn, like a phoenix rising from the ashes."

1.12 INFAMY

AIRED January 11, 2012
WRITTEN BY Dan Dworkin and Jay Beattie
DIRECTED BY Matt Earl Beesley

With the Grayson divorce getting uglier, Emily sets her sights on another target, author Mason Treadwell.

Fire. It's one of the two "primal bookends" Victoria will choose as the theme for Emily and Daniel's upcoming engagement party, but it isn't until "Infamy" that we learn how apt that theme is for Emily. Not only is it strongly suggested in this episode that young Amanda Clarke was an arsonist, Emily uses fire as her weapon of choice in her takedown of the journalist who betrayed her trust as a young girl: Mason Treadwell, author of *The Society Connection*, the book that failed to out the Graysons' conspiracy against David Clarke.

Treadwell is only the latest in the line of Emily's targets to use the Grayson conspiracy to their own personal advantage, but Treadwell may be the worst of all — at least in Emily's eyes. Unlike Emily's other targets and the Graysons, who are trying to put the past behind them, Treadwell is reveling in it. He's still giving talks about the book that made his career almost 15 years ago. He not only saved the Clarke tapes, he has them on display in his home. And now he's writing a book about writing the book that made his career. David Clarke's downfall gives his life purpose. In many ways, Mason is like Fauxmanda. Neither is intrinsically linked to the David Clarke saga, but by being connected to it, they create new identities, new histories, and new futures: Treadwell as a respected literary icon, Fauxmanda as the love of Jack's life.

Emily literally destroys Treadwell's home and life's work in an effort to move forward with her plan to destroy the Graysons' household — which is already fracturing thanks to Victoria and Conrad's divorce proceedings and Charlotte and Daniel's ventures outside of the Grayson fold. The more Charlotte and Daniel push away from their parents, the more Victoria and Conrad try to keep them close. But this is more than your standard empty nest syndrome: the kids are straight-up being used to gain leverage as the divorce progresses. As a result of Victoria and Conrad's moves against each other, Daniel's best card to play is proposing to Emily and leaving the nest altogether — the exact opposite of what either of parent wants for their son.

Though Fauxmanda successfully weathers her tiff with Jack about what's appropriate behavior at the Stowaway, she is about to encounter a bigger storm. Emily has set her up to take a big fall, framed as the fire-starting wild child who acted on her threat against Treadwell. Emily's willing to let Fauxmanda become as infamous as her father if it means getting what she wants done. As Nolan would say, "Bad girl."

BEST SERVED COLD It's been a while since Emily completed a true takedown of an original target. Watching her walk away from Treadwell's burning cottage is almost as satisfying as watching him bawling like a baby while Nolan smugly looks on.

HAMPTONS HOMAGE *The Dangerous Summer*, published posthumously in 1985, is Hemingway's last book. While the plot offers little insight into the world of *Revenge*, the fact that Hemingway wrote his last book in that cottage is a nice little bit of foreshadowing that Treadwell's own career will soon be over.

Mason Treadwell owns John Cheever's typewriter. Cheever, considered one of the greatest American short fiction writers of the 20th-century, often wrote about the duality found in human nature. Stories such as "The Enormous Radio," "The Five-Forty-Eight," and "The Swimmer" feature characters whose public personas greatly conflict with their inner turmoil, which is not only an apt writing device for Mason Treadwell, a man whose career was made on creating a new persona, but also apt for the subjects that he writes about. The Graysons' public image contradicts the reality that they were complicit in the bombing of Flight 197. David Clarke's public persona is that of an evil terrorist, but he was nothing more than a loving father destroyed by those he trusted.

WHO'S THAT GUY? If Mason Treadwell seems a tad theatrical, you can thank Roger Bart's background for that. Bart gave a Tony-winning performance of Snoopy in the Broadway revival of *You're a Good Man, Charlie Brown* (1999), originated the role of Carmen Ghia in *The Producers* (2001–2007), and originated the role of Dr. Frankenstein in Mel Brooks' *Young Frankenstein* (2007–2009). He's no stranger to *Desperate Housewives* fans either. Bart played Bree's mentally unstable pharmacist-turned-lover George Williams in the second season (2005–2006). *Special bonus trivia:* Before his Victoria Grayson–funded makeover, Mason Treadwell went by the name Leo Treadwell; Roger Bart took on the role of the unassuming and nervous accountant Leo Bloom during *The Producers'* Broadway run.

BORROWED FROM THE BOOK When Dantès discovers his neighbor Caderousse after all these years, he decides to give Caderousse a chance to redeem himself and offers him one-fifth of a diamond. Caderousse, ever the opportunist, tries to take the entire diamond instead. In the end, Dantès punishes him for his greed. Like Dantès' offering to Caderousse, Emily gives Mason the opportunity to right his past wrongs at the private reading at Victoria's home. But professional and social advancement mean more to Treadwell than doing the right thing and he takes advantage of the situation, which only leads him to ruin.

BEHIND THE SCENES Mason Treadwell's fashion sense is a deliberate and direct reference to another non-fiction writer who infiltrated New York's upper crust society: Truman Capote. "He has access to a lot of different styles and information; he's very, very creative," costume designer Jill Ohanneson said of Treadwell. This gave them room to play with color and distinct accessories in new ways. "We had a great time doing the whole episode, but he was our all-around favorite, definitely."

REVENGENDA How will the knowledge that Charlotte is her half-sister affect Emily's plans for revenge? Will Jack really be able to lighten up? What will Victoria choose: losing her share of Grayson Global to Conrad or losing Daniel to Emily? Why didn't David share the info about Charlotte's paternity in his journals?

REVENGESPIRATION
"Bad things happen to good people." — young Amanda Clarke

REVENGE READING
JOHN MILTON'S *PARADISE LOST*

Charlotte's first school reading assignment takes her all the way back to the fall of man. John Milton's *Paradise Lost*, first published in 1667, is the re-telling of the story of Adam and Eve, in the form of a 12-part epic poem à la Homer's *Odyssey* and *Iliad*.

In *Paradise Lost*, Adam and Eve are God's ultimate creations. Satan, the original sinner, decides to corrupt these perfect creatures by convincing them to eat from the Tree of Knowledge. He succeeds, and Adam and Eve are sent away from the Garden of Eden. Through these characters, *Paradise Lost* suggests there are two paths we can choose from after sinning: a lifetime seeking redemption (as Adam and Eve choose) or a lifetime of sin (as Satan chooses). These are the two paths Emily Thorne must choose from: her path to redemption is via "absolute forgiveness" and her sinful path is through "moral vindication." However, as *Paradise Lost* demonstrates, neither path results in a sense of satisfaction. Adam and Eve never redeem humankind from original sin and Satan becomes more paranoid and delusional.

At its core, the story of Satan, Adam, and Eve is a story of revenge. Satan corrupts Adam and Eve as payback for being kicked out of heaven by God. Satan creates temptation for Adam and Eve, and they choose to give into it — which is exactly what Emily does to take her targets down. They yield to temptation and are then punished for it. Even though Adam and Eve can be blamed for their own fall, Satan struggles with his decision to harm the innocent. He never is fully satisfied with the outcome. As Milton writes, "Revenge, at first though sweet, / Bitter ere long back on it self recoils." Satan's revenge has unintended consequences for himself and for all of humanity. The short-term gain of his revenge (getting Adam and Eve kicked out of the Garden of Eden) pales in comparison to the long-term fall-out of his revenge (he never gets back into heaven, he becomes increasingly marginalized, and all of humanity suffers eternally because of Adam and Eve). The conclusion of *Paradise Lost* is that while the path to redemption is a long, hard road, it is more satisfying than sin, which has instant gratification but more negative consequences.

Which leaves Emily Thorne with quite the dilemma. Does she follow Satan's path and continue down her path of revenge, lose herself in the process, and create more problems than she anticipated? Or does she follow Adam and Eve and do her best to forgive, knowing that, as a fallible creature, she lacks the capacity to do so completely and absolutely?

• ● •

"Some say that our lives are defined by the sum of our choices. But it isn't really our choices that distinguish who we are, but our commitment to them."

1.13 COMMITMENT

AIRED January 18, 2012
WRITTEN BY Mark B. Perry and Liz Tigelaar
DIRECTED BY Kenneth Fink

Daniel proposes to Emily; she considers saying no and putting her revenge plans on hold. That doesn't last long, thanks to Victoria.

As Conrad and Victoria's commitment to their marriage collapses, Daniel and Emily make a commitment of their own. Neither of Daniel's parents is particularly thrilled about this prospect, and Conrad tries to tell Daniel that the puppy love of a new relationship isn't enough of a foundation on which to build a life. And he should know. In many ways, Daniel and Emily's courtship parallels Conrad and Victoria's. A

successful man chooses to follow his heart, while a mysterious, alluring woman cons him into marriage, offering him everything his current family doesn't.

Both of these relationships are built on lies. Even when Victoria makes a decision that's rooted in honest emotion — carrying the child of the man she loves or telling the truth to her son — it's clouded by her desire for self-preservation. She didn't actively try to convince Conrad that Charlotte was his child or flat-out lie to Daniel by saying David Clarke raped her. Instead, she manipulates the emotional landscape so that they come to those conclusions on their own. In order to protect herself, Victoria projects an image that satisfies a relationship's needs. Conrad wanted a dutiful loving wife; Daniel wants an honest and loving mother. Victoria can play the parts — but only a discerning audience can see just how much it's a performance.

Emily is also a master of manipulating the truth to obtain an emotional advantage. For each of her takedowns, Emily orchestrates situations where the truth will out for people to interpret as they see fit. However, these maneuvers result in a big pile of collateral damage that's weighing down on her conscience. Emily, like Victoria, wants to lift this emotional weight by protecting the ones she loves. But even an act of protection provides a personal advantage for these two. Emily spirits Fauxmanda out of town to protect her and Jack, but doing so safeguards her revenge plan. She apologizes to Nolan, but doing so means she has him on-side as her faithful assistant.

As a result of their meddling, Victoria gets to keep her social status and family and Emily gets to keep her plans on track. Emily and Victoria both have made big commitments that have defined their lives — Victoria to upholding the Grayson name, Emily to avenging the Clarke name — but in the end, their ultimate commitment is to themselves. And as long as they continue to get in each other's way, viewers can expect quite the showdown.

BEST SERVED COLD With as little as a look Victoria let Daniel think David raped her. That betrays not only her son but the man she loved.

HAMPTONS HOMAGE Nolan calls Fauxmanda "Chatty Cathy," a popular talking doll made by Mattel that was sold from 1959 to 1965. Nolan's nickname for her refers not only to the fact that Fauxmanda said too much about Emily and the Graysons to Jack, but that Fauxmanda is merely Emily's toy.

BEHIND THE SCENES Conrad Grayson has been pretty scary so far, but also pretty absent when it comes to fathering his children. This changes with Daniel's plan to marry Emily. Henry Czerny was excited to see his character's growth. He's especially proud of the complex reaction Conrad has to the engagement news. "He exposes a side of himself that he wishes he could expose more often and share more often but doesn't," Czerny said to *Xfinity*. "So I love the arc of that scene."

REVENGENDA Will we see Fauxmanda again? Why is the SEC "sniffing around" Grayson Global? Will Ashley plan Daniel and Emily's wedding? Will Charlotte find out about her true paternity? Will Conrad ever again think of Charlotte as his own daughter? And what is Ashley going to do with all her overheard information?

REVENGESPIRATION
"You think one storm has passed and another one is on the horizon." — Daniel Grayson

FASHION
ON *REVENGE*

For the rich and famous, it's often not *what* you're wearing, but *who* you're wearing that matters. And the wealthy that inhabit the world of *Revenge* are no exception. From Victoria's bandage dresses to Nolan's double popped collar, every piece of clothing that makes it on-screen is carefully selected to convey the Hamptons lifestyle: effortless, immaculate, and dirty rich.

Costume designer Jill Ohanneson and her team make the clothing selections for *Revenge*. After they receive the script, they meet with the producer and director and discuss the feeling they want to convey that week. They look at their current collection of clothing and make a list for each character of what they already have and what they need to buy. Then they hit the road to shop. Once the clothing is acquired, they assemble the outfits and do fittings with the cast. Sometimes the clothes work, sometimes they don't. When they do, the producer and director working on that episode must approve them. After alterations, each piece of clothing and all the accessories are ready to make their TV debut.

When Victoria made the declaration "no more bandage dresses" to Ashley in "Infamy," it felt as though she was speaking to the fans who have commented on her staple style: flattering but (very!) fitted dresses designed by Herve Leger. Victoria wears such a dress in almost every episode. With tight, expensive dresses that are usually in rich jewel tones, Victoria "dresses to intimidate," Ohanneson said. "Victoria states her intentions with what she is wearing." When she wants to be in control, she'll don a bandage dress, the tight fit reflecting how she wishes to control her world. When she wants to stand out, she wears magenta while everyone else is in pastels, like at the mother/daughter tea in "Duplicity." When she wants to signal a fresh start for the Graysons, she asks for them all to don white, as at Emily and Daniel's engagement photo shoot. Established houses like Dolce & Gabbana, Christian Dior, and Carolina Herrera designed most of Victoria's pieces. Victoria, as a woman of status and power, wants the names she wears to have the appropriate status and power in the fashion world. "She's very aware of the impact she has on the people around her," Madeleine Stowe said, and her wardrobe reflects that.

While Victoria dresses to stand out, Emily Thorne dresses to blend in. Her clothes are often unassuming and modest. "We want to kind of keep Emily clean, so that nobody ever expects that she is doing what she is doing," Ohanneson said. "It's all an illusion." This illusion includes a lot of neutrals and elegant designers that evoke timeless class, wealth, and elegance like Fendi, Oscar de la Renta, Valentino, Michael Kors, and Gucci. Emily dresses relatively mature for her age, and that's a deliberate decision as well. She wants to come across as marriage material, someone whose first impression says "wealthy, responsible neighbor." Grace Kelly is the main source of inspiration for Ohanneson's team when styling Emily. "The key is all these simple yet elegant lines," Ohanneson said. "She's a little bit more demure, a little more preppy."

Victoria and Emily may have the most costume changes, but they aren't the only fashion stars on *Revenge*. Never content to be one behind-the-scenes, Ashley Davenport is often seen in bright, bold colors and trendy designers, showcasing the fact that she's forward thinking and creative (essential for party planners) and doesn't want to get lost in the crowd (essential for aspiring social climbers). She knows how to "edge it up a little" Ashley Madekwe said. She also knows how to find the best buys, Ohanneson said, making the most of the pittance the Graysons give her, and the costume department's choices reflect that.

The character who has most set the fashion world a-buzz isn't any one of the lovely ladies. It's Nolan

Ross, whose carefully constructed wardrobe represents a Hamptons that exists only in his mind. "Nolan's fashion is off-beat and a little off-kilter," Ohanneson said. "He has the money to buy anything that he wants, any fashion, any clothing, no matter what the price, but he never can quite put it together." Or he puts it together too well; those polo shirt–matching pocket squares and patterned socks don't go unnoticed. Most of all, the costume department is having fun with Nolan. As Gabriel Mann said, "He definitely likes to express himself in the way that he dresses."

Every costume change and accessory choice on *Revenge* has a purpose and tells a story of its own. "People say it's a story about forgiveness," costume supervisor Sandy Kenyon said. "I say it's a story about clothes."

• ● •

"Truth is a battle of perceptions. People only see what they are prepared to confront. It's not what you look at that matters, but what you see."

1.14 PERCEPTION

AIRED February 8, 2012
WRITTEN BY Nikki Toscano and Sallie Patrick
DIRECTED BY Tim Hunter

Grandpa Grayson is in town to celebrate Daniel and Emily's engagement and to protect his company from the fall-out of Conrad and Victoria's divorce. Meanwhile, Jack deals with the fall-out of Fauxmanda's sudden disappearance and the sudden appearance of a Treadwell tape under his bed.

"Perception" is an appropriate title for an episode of *Revenge*, because, at the end of the day, it's perception that Emily depends on for her plans to work. She needs her targets to see her as her assumed identity, a wealthy orphaned philanthropist socialite desperately in love with Daniel, and nothing more. When people perceive her differently — or, worse, for who she really is — things fall apart.

As Emily continues to balance her assumed identity with who she really is, Fauxmanda faces the same battle. Ever since she adopted the name Amanda Clarke and showed up in the Hamptons, she's struggled with who she wants to be and how to fit that person into the Hamptons' social landscape. But Fauxmanda faces another perception problem: the expectations Jack has of "Amanda Clarke." For Jack, Amanda represents happiness, innocence, and unsullied love and loyalty. But this present-day Amanda has a dark past and a tendency for arson and theft. Jack can't reconcile his idealized image of Amanda with this new reality of her.

While Fauxmanda is trying to live up to an imagined version of Amanda Clarke, Daniel is doing everything he can to separate himself from the Grayson name. He's tried different ways to kick the connotations of being a Grayson: by being a party boy, by working at the bar, or by being a dedicated fiancé. But his fallback identity as Daniel Grayson, son of Conrad and Victoria, the next CEO of Grayson Global, has always been there for him, making it safe for him to be rebellious. Charlotte, on the other hand, has always struggled to fit into her family. Her mother was always cold and distant, her father, while loving, was rarely around. Now she has a reason to explain her inability to fluidly fit into her family. Charlotte has been hit with an identity-shattering truth — she has the Grayson name but not the Grayson genes. How will her perception of herself change in the wake of this bombshell?

Conrad has daddy issues of his own to deal with. His father believes he is no longer capable of running Grayson Global and that he's become too caught up in propagating a perception of a happy family that he's forgotten to work toward making that perception a reality. Conrad and his father's relationship offers interesting insight into how Conrad fathers his own children. While Grandpa Grayson insists that personal happiness is more important that public perception, he convinces Charlotte of the opposite: he'd rather see his granddaughter continue doing drugs than compromise the family company. Conrad has adopted this hands-off, company-first parenting approach as well, and the result is a family whose battles become more public the nastier they get. But Conrad hates being underestimated, and when he sees a challenge, he'll rise to it. Does this mean he'll fight to prove to Charlotte that being a father means more than sharing DNA? And will he finally do what his father says — and not what his father does — and try to fix his family?

This tension between self-perception and reality is a problem for all of the characters, and there's a gap between who they are and who they aspire to be. Nolan is Emily's confidant, but wants to be Jack's friend. Daniel is a Grayson, but wants to be his own man. Ashley is Victoria's lackey, but wants to be a Hamptons power player. Jack is Fauxmanda's "alibi," but wants to be her saving grace. Emily is a scheming revenger, but wants to be some people's protectors. Conrad is not Charlotte's biological father, but wants to be there for her. And Victoria is rejected by her children, but wants nothing more than to be back in their good graces.

BEST SERVED COLD Jack finally steps up and takes control! No one speaks like that to Victoria, and watching him unveil her secrets is a delight. He kicks off the most exciting dinner party the Graysons have had in quite a while, one that begins with an aggressive accusation and ends with a startling revelation.

WHO'S THAT GUY? William Devane (Edward Grayson) is American soap royalty. The actor spent 10 years playing scheming senator Greg Sumner on the *Dallas* spin-off *Knots Landing* (1983–1993). Fans of Tom Selleck's Jesse Stone mysteries will recognize Devane as Dr. Dix and *24* fans should be pleased to see Secretary of Defense James Heller back on their screens (2005–2007). Devane has over 40 years of acting experience under his belt, including roles in movies like Alfred Hitchcock's *Family Plot* (1976), *Marathon Man* (1976) with Dustin Hoffman, and *Payback* (1999) with Mel Gibson. *Special bonus trivia:* Like Edward Grayson,

© IZUMI HASEGAWA / PR PHOTOS

166 best served cold

Greg Sumner loves the ladies, romancing several of his neighbors, co-workers, and employees.

BORROWED FROM THE BOOK Just as Emily tries to shelter Charlotte by not revealing who her father is, Dantès decides to protect Valentine. Dantès puts a stop to the poisoning of Valentine and helps her discover who is trying to kill her and why. As characters reveal themselves to be better than their guilty parents or loved ones, Dantès' plans become more complicated. He tries to protect those he has grown fond of while still taking down his targets — the same problem Emily struggles with as she becomes fonder of Daniel and Charlotte.

REVENGENDA Was Emily really driven to back off her plan because of Nolan's morality lesson? What will Charlotte do now that she knows she's not a Grayson? Will Daniel really become CEO of Grayson Global? How will Victoria win back her children? Who stole the infinity box — and what does it mean for Emily?

REVENGESPIRATION
"Don't let the place you start dictate the place you finish." — Edward Grayson

REVENGE READING
WILLIAM BLAKE'S
THE MARRIAGE OF HEAVEN AND HELL

"If the doors of perception were cleansed, everything would appear to man as it is, infinite." The first time Emily ever sees Daniel, he's in a bar trying to win over some girl — and explain his entire existence — by drunkenly quoting poetry. Little did he know that not only would that moment solidify his fate, he was setting the stage for his family's destruction and a very special episode of *Revenge*.

Originally written in 1790, William Blake's *The Marriage of Heaven and Hell* explores the many themes and characters from the Bible that have infiltrated Western thought, especially the notion that good and evil and sin and redemption are opposing concepts, that people must strive for one or the other. (In fact, Blake wrote it as a direct response to *Paradise Lost*, which Charlotte was assigned to read in "Infamy.") Blake argues these concepts are not diametrically opposed, but rather work together to form humanity, a flawed but glorious existence. *Revenge*, like Blake's work, demonstrates that it is impossible for people to be singularly good or evil. There is no absolute, only perception. From Victoria's perspective, her actions are justifiable; from Emily's, they are not — but her own are.

The Bible suggests that reason (which inspires people to be more God-like) takes precedence over energy (which inspires people to sin). Blake suggests this may be the case, but some of the most fun aspects of being human require energy. To be driven solely by reason will lead to a fundamentally boring life. (Looking at you, Jack.) And thus, we need both aspects to fully understand, appreciate, and take advantage of being human. Let's face it: Emily may be a bad girl, but she sure is fun to watch.

• ● •

"The best way to fight chaos is with chaos."

1.15 CHAOS

AIRED February 15, 2012
WRITTEN BY Mark Fish and Joe Fazzio
DIRECTED BY Sanford Bookstaver

At Emily and Daniel's engagement party, someone gets shot and more questions get asked than answered.

Chaos theory is about understanding the order in the most disordered systems. Tyler is dead and Daniel is looking like a prime suspect; the Hamptons and Emily's plans are in a state of chaos. In chaos theory, the outcome is always determined by the initial conditions. If you look at what went down at Daniel and Emily's engagement party, each participant is largely driven by pre-existing conditions: Daniel and his difficult relationship with his parents; Victoria and her insecurity; Fauxmanda and her intense neediness and loyalty to Emily; Jack and his vulnerability and yearning for Amanda; Nolan and his ability to emotionally manipulate; Tyler and his mental instability and anger; and Takeda and his lack of faith in Emily. Emily's lies, big and small, simply set the system in motion.

The three people shaken up the most by the events leading up to the engagement party are Tyler, Fauxmanda, and Jack. Tyler may be off his medication (which adds to his crazy), but it must be infuriating to come back to the Hamptons and see that not only does no one miss him, someone else has managed to execute the plan he had in mind, pretending to be someone else to become essential to the Graysons. Fauxmanda wants proof that her relationship with Emily is real and as important to Emily as it is to her. Instead, there's enough evidence of Emily's betrayal that Fauxmanda easily believes Tyler, her own suspicions and insecurities fueled by his argument. But she's just as easily brought back to Emily's side with the news that Emily framed Tyler and encouraged her relationship with Jack. It's what Fauxmanda *wants* to be true.

And Jack, well, Jack wants nothing more than love. Any opportunity that gives him that possibility, he's there, with an open heart and open mind. In some ways, Tyler's ambition, Fauxmanda's loyalty, and Jack's big heart are their biggest strengths. But under the wrong conditions, they become their greatest weaknesses.

In chaos theory, a small change in a system yields wildly different outcomes. We know Emily's lies get the ball rolling, but events quickly snowball beyond her control. Which leaves us to make sense of the chaos: we know Tyler is dead. We don't know who killed him. While some evidence rules certain people out (Emily was at the party, Jack heard the shot from the car, Nolan is terrible with a gun), it's feasible that any number of characters could have pulled the trigger. After the upheaval of the recent past, it's difficult to say who's capable of murder. Who shot Tyler? And why?

Emily better find out fast if she wants to regain control of this chaotic system.

BEST SERVED COLD At the Fire and Ice party, Victoria lets her claws out. Her so-nice-it-wasn't-nice-at-all engagement speech sets the tone for her relationship with her future daughter-in-law. Emily, Conrad, and everyone else who heard it know that Victoria won't go down without a fight.

HAMPTONS HOMAGE Conrad would rather sit next to the Paulsons at the party. Perhaps he's referring to the family of John Paulson, a hedge fund manager who is the founder and president of Paulson & Co., based in New York. In 2010, he set a hedge fund record by making nearly $5 billion by selling subprime mortgages, but the company lost big in 2011 when it made a series of bad trades.

BEHIND THE SCENES In "Chaos," we finally get back to the Fire and Ice Ball that opened the pilot. While everything appears the same as it was in that flashforward, looks can be deceiving. The entire party was re-shot for "Chaos." Why? First, Tyler and Fauxmanda's storylines didn't yet exist (although Mike Kelley said that he intended to keep Daniel alive from the very beginning). Second, director Sanford Bookstaver wanted to reinforce the idea that perception matters. He wanted the audience to see "the same scenes from a different perspective, subtly, just enough to make a difference." It took a lot of work to make it happen, as the shooting schedule for "Chaos" was only nine days, as opposed to the 12 they had for the pilot. "I had to study the pilot and the script, and I had to map out a blueprint of it all," Bookstaver told *Entertainment Weekly*. "We had to rebuild that entire Fire and Ice tent. We went back to the beach. We had everybody in the same wardrobes. It was really complicated."

REVENGENDA How did Tyler find Fauxmanda? How did Takeda discover Tyler's secret hideout? How did he know Tyler had the infinity box — and his own plan for revenge? How does Takeda know Nolan? Where is Takeda taking Fauxmanda? What will happen to Daniel now that his hands are literally covered in blood?

REVENGESPIRATION
"Blood will always be thicker than water." — Victoria Grayson

WHAT'S IN A NAME?

Like everything else on *Revenge*, the names of the characters are rife with meaning.

Emily: Not only is Emily the "thorn" in the Graysons' side, she's Victoria's biggest rival and adversary — which is apt considering Emily means "rival."

Amanda: Emily's given name, Amanda, means "she who is loved." Many people, especially her father and Jack, love Amanda unconditionally.

David: David means "beloved," fitting for a man beloved by both his daughter and Victoria. Interestingly, his wife's name, Kara, also means "beloved," perhaps signifying that Emily loves her mother just as much as she loves her father.

Victoria: Victoria Grayson is a warrior, and she tends to win most of her battles, living up to her name, which means "conqueror." Victoria's name is also a homage to *Revenge*'s soapy predecessor *Dallas*. Victoria Principal played Pamela Ewing, whose second fiancé was named Mark Graison.

Conrad: Conrad is the "bold ruler" of the Grayson household and of Grayson Global. But his given name hints at his darker side. Even Henry Czerny acknowledges there is more than a passing resemblance between Conrad Grayson and Conrad Black, the newspaper magnate convicted of financial fraud and obstruction of justice in 2007.

Daniel: Daniel means "God is my judge," an appropriate name for a man who wants to be judged on his merits as a person and not by his family or money.

Charlotte: All Charlotte wants is to be free of the trappings of her family and their burdens, which shouldn't surprise anyone since her name means "free man."

Nolan: Nolan is always trying to get Emily to do the "noble" thing and follow her heart. Nolan's name is yet another nod to the soap operas that influenced *Revenge*. It seems fitting that the most fashionable character on the show would share a name with Nolan Miller, *Dynasty*'s costume designer, the man responsible for Joan Collins's iconic shoulder pads.

Jack: Jack is the moral center of *Revenge*, and his given name reflects that. Jack means "God is gracious," suitable for a man who tries to find the good in everything.

Declan: Declan (and Connor Paolo's inconsistent accent) winks at the Porters' working-class Irish heritage, but the name also means "full of goodness." Declan is one of the few truly good characters, trying his best to protect Charlotte and his brother from hurting themselves.

Ashley: Ashley is Ashley Madekwe's first name and Mike Kelley named the character after her. Her last name, Davenport, is a nod to the Brit who starred on Mike Kelley's other show, *Swingtown*. Actor Jack Davenport played futures trader Bruce Miller on *Swingtown* and is known for films such as *Pirates of the Caribbean* and *The Talented Mr. Ripley*.

Tyler: Tyler means "tile-maker" or "tile-layer." Tiles make mosaics, patterns made out of random bits and pieces of other tiles. Tyler has constructed his life in much the same way a mosaic is constructed: using bits and pieces of others' lives and of straight-up lies to create a believable Harvard buddy for Daniel.

• ● •

"A conflicted heart feeds on doubt and confusion.
It will make you question your path,
your tactics, your motives."

1.16 SCANDAL

AIRED February 29, 2012
WRITTEN BY Elle Triedman
DIRECTED BY Kenneth Fink

In the aftermath of Tyler's murder, attention on the Graysons heats up and Daniel is charged with the crime.

In the midst of a scandal, the person at the eye of the storm needs support most of all. When it all goes to hell, who do you lean on? Who do you trust? And who do you throw under the bus?

Despite the recent rift with Victoria, Daniel turns to his mother, honoring her command to not say a word to the point of possibly incriminating himself. Despite the pressure to do otherwise, Daniel obeys his mother, and by doing so, he demonstrates his loyalty to her — and Victoria is a proven powerhouse in a time of crisis — while biding his time to figure out what happened on the beach and how much loyalty Emily deserves from him.

Tyler, despite his recent history of craziness with the Graysons, has cast doubt in Daniel's mind about Emily armed with only a photo and a gun. Either Daniel is almost as gullible as Fauxmanda, or Daniel already had some doubt about Emily that he chose to ignore. Scandals can smarten someone up, and Daniel attempts to evaluate his situation with clear eyes. A scandal can also be an opportunity — and Ashley seizes her moment, playing the supportive aide-de-camp while underhandedly working her own angle.

Conrad points out that the Graysons are reliving their past, once again caught up in a scandal that captures the public's imagination. If only Conrad knew *just* how right he is. Daniel, like David Clarke before him, is privileged but fundamentally moral; he wants a simple life with the woman he loves. But when she refused to run away (because she was unwilling to turn her back on her personal agenda), he finds himself at the center of a conspiracy far greater than he can fathom.

While the Graysons solidify their loyalties to each other, Emily is left questioning where hers lie. Nolan betrays her by secretly working with Takeda; Takeda meddles in her plans; and her feelings for Jack, Daniel, and now half-sis Charlotte are muddying her path. The engagement party was the first time we saw Emily break, and she wants to get control back. That's why even though she could just walk away — an action that would add to the public presumption of Daniel's guilt — and watch the Grayson empire burn down, she won't. Though the Graysons suffer in seeing their beloved son in jail imprisoned for a violent crime, in discovering their daughter hates them and has turned to drugs to cope, and in witnessing their company disparaged in the press, from Emily's perspective, the scales of justice are not in balance. Their suffering does not weigh up to what they did to David Clarke. As she said in the first episode, "Two wrongs can never equal each other."

Which means that Emily must have something in store for them that is much, much worse.

BEST SERVED COLD Even when the family needs as much support as it can get, Victoria can't help but slip in a not-so-passive aggressive dig at Emily. Victoria saying to Emily that "Maybe your time in the juvenile detention facility will end up being an asset in Daniel's court case" is the best line of the episode.

HAMPTONS HOMAGE Nolan welcomes Jack into the "cone of silence," a term coined as part of a recurring joke in *Get Smart*, a 1960s comedy series about an incompetent spy unit. Not only is this a sly nod to many secretive and spy-like elements to *Revenge*, it also references how madcap and amateur Emily's entire mission can be. It's Emily, Nolan, some bad disguises, a clichéd Japanese sensei, the "homicidal stripper version of Whac-a-mole," a whale cam, and an immortal dog. Put that together and it sounds more like a comedy series than a spy thriller.

While the "Who Shot Tyler?" question was answered quickly, no soap would feel complete without at least one mysterious murder by gunshot, thanks to the most famous soap storyline of all time, *Dallas*'s "Who Shot J.R.?"

WHO'S THAT GUY? Veronica Cartwright (Judge Elizabeth Blackwell) is best known for her 1970s sci-fi films *Invasion of the Body Snatchers* (1978) and *Alien* (1979). Since then, Cartwright has kept busy, primarily on television, earning Emmy nominations for her guest roles on *ER* (1997) and *The X-Files* (1998–1999).

Revenge isn't the first time Courtney B. Vance (Benjamin Brooks) played a powerful attorney. He did so on *Law & Order: Criminal Intent*, where he starred as assistant district attorney Ron Carver for five seasons (2001–2006). More recently, Vance was seen as FBI agent Stanford Wedeck on the short-lived ABC show *FlashForward* (2009–2010).

BEHIND THE SCENES Do you think Jack is being obsessive about his need to find Fauxmanda? Nick Wechsler doesn't think so. If he found himself in the same situation as Jack — his girlfriend standing over a body, then taking off without any explanation — he'd want answers too. "I'd be like, 'Tell me everything!,'" Wechsler said to *After Elton*. "Just knowing what it is that we're involved in explains a lot but I still need to hear it from you,' and I need to know that she's okay."

REVENGENDA How will Daniel handle Rikers? What will Nolan do with his new information about Ashley? Will Emily help Charlotte understand her father? Why did Takeda kill Tyler, but not Daniel? What's his game plan?

REVENGESPIRATION
"No matter how we try to escape our past, we seem destined to repeat it." — Conrad Grayson

REVENGE READING
F. SCOTT FITZGERALD'S *THE GREAT GATSBY*

Marty Bowen revealed that when they were looking for ideas while developing their new Hamptons-set show, one of the first sources they considered was F. Scott Fitzgerald's classic novel *The Great Gatsby*. While the concept didn't work, *Gatsby*-ian influences have made their way into *Revenge* in other ways.

First published in 1925, *The Great Gatsby* is set in the middle of the Roaring '20s, the summer of 1922, one of the most prosperous times in American history. Nick Carraway is a recent Yale graduate and World War I veteran who moves to New York City in pursuit of the American dream. He rents a house on Long Island's North Shore, near his cousin Daisy and her husband, Tom, and right next door to the mysterious Jay Gatsby, known for throwing the neighborhood's most extravagant parties.

Like Nick, Emily is a newcomer to the world where elite New Yorkers summer and moves in next door to the most infamous house on the block, Grayson Manor. The Graysons, like Gatsby, are known for their lavish parties and have accrued their wealth, in part, through mysterious and criminal means. Victoria reinvented herself as the most upper crust of Hamptons society, just like Jay Gatsby did. Victoria earned her place in the upper crust, while Gatsby always remained an outsider — much like Nolan Ross. Both command attention but never quite fit in, despite their extreme measures to do so: Jay with his parties, Nolan with his wardrobe (he would love Gatsby's shirt collection), and both with their giant homes.

Both *Revenge* and *The Great Gatsby* center on a love affair gone wrong and are concerned with wealth and the problems it fosters. In *The Great Gatsby*, Fitzgerald explores how the American Dream changed after the first World War and how sudden prosperity made material goods matter to some people much more than the ideals America was based on: hard work, individualism, health, and happiness. *Revenge* explores the American Dream from the opposite arc. The economy is collapsing and people like the Graysons are scrambling to hold on to the possessions that have come to define the American Dream: big houses, fancy cars, and designer clothes. As the Grayson lifestyle comes under increasing scrutiny thanks to a series of scandals (helpfully set up by Emily), Victoria begins to realize the danger of her priorities. Victoria could have been happy if she'd followed her heart, instead of compromising herself in the pursuit of money, social status, and power.

In *The Great Gatsby*, that lesson comes too late, if at all, for many of Fitzgerald's characters, and the modern-day Hamptons elite seem poised to face the same fate.

● ● ●

*"Doubt is a disease. It infects the mind
creating a mistrust of people's motives
and of one's own perceptions."*

1.17 DOUBT

AIRED April 18, 2012
STORY BY Mike Kelley
TELEPLAY BY Dan Dwokin and Jay Beattie
DIRECTED BY Matt Earl Beesley

With Daniel in jail, the Graysons are trying to find someone else to pin Tyler's murder on, while Emily hunts down Victoria's lackey to get information, and Victoria gets Daniel beat up in order to bring him home.

Tyler's death resulted in chaos throughout the Hamptons, and as the dust settles, those involved are left to take stock of what happened and do their best to take control of how it all gets cleaned up.

It took a few crazy events, but Emily is back in control. She's approached the fall-out from Tyler's murder like a cold-blooded, er, killer. Control freak that she is, Emily's identified her weaknesses (her feelings for Jack and Daniel) and wants to right the wrongs her weaknesses created to get back on the revenge track.

Part of getting things done her way is shielding Jack from harm, hence the wild good chase after Fauxmanda. Emily's not alone in protecting the eldest Porter: Declan also takes action to right his wrongs and protect his big bro. Since their father's death, Declan has relied on Jack for emotional and financial support, but hasn't been particularly appreciative. Now he has a high-stakes opportunity to return the favor as Jack focuses on Fauxmanda's fate instead of his own, and Declan is jumping on the chance, even if it means hurting Charlotte.

In order for Declan to help Jack, he turns to someone who has more power than he does: Mason Treadwell. Thanks to Emily's manipulation, Mason is back in the game. He gets to control the narrative that the

Daniel Grayson trial takes. Like Declan, Emily, and Victoria counting on controlling Mason to spin the story the way they want, Mason uses this opportunity to take control of his career and separate himself from the Graysons' stranglehold. He's well aware that Declan is using him to help his brother, but by agreeing to tell Declan's story, Mason sends a very strong message to Victoria and the rest of the world: from now on, no one controls Mason Treadwell.

Emily, Declan, and Mason aren't the only ones asserting themselves. So is Daniel. In a weird way, being in jail and charged with murder gives Daniel what he wanted: an identity separate from his parents. It's given him the strength to stand up

© TINA GILL / PR PHOTOS

to his mother and the strength to take the fall if it means protecting his loved ones, especially Emily. It finally shows Victoria that he's not the perfect son she makes him out to be. Incarcerated, he has the freedom to make his own mistakes and take control of his own destiny.

Meanwhile, Victoria, Jack, and Charlotte are losing control. Charlotte tries to reclaim control by acting out: she's glib about what she saw on the beach, cuts Declan out of her life, takes pills, and talks back to Mason Treadwell and her mother. Victoria goes to new lengths to get a handle on things: she slaps her daughter, hires someone to beat up her son just to spring him from jail, and runs into the arms of a former lover. Victoria knows how devastating this affair could be to the Grayson public image, and thus to Daniel's case. If the roles were reversed and Conrad was sleeping around, she'd have none of it. Victoria believes she may lose the one thing in life she truly loves — her son — and is doing her best to deal with it. As a result, she turns to the only other person she's loved (and who's still alive): Dominik. She, like Charlotte, feels alone, unwanted, and out of control. It's a position that is as dangerous as it is powerful, and those in control better watch out.

BEST SERVED COLD Emily served it up to Lee Moran in the alley behind the bar. Watching her kick the crap out of Victoria's thug, then declare her allegiance to both Jack and Daniel, *then* take an imprint of his car key proves the girl is back on her game.

HAMPTONS HOMAGE Nolan is worried that Takeda might "release the Kraken," a legendary sea monster believed to live off the coast of Norway and Greenland. This reference reinforces the many nautical and dark themes *Revenge* shares with *Moby-Dick*: that the unknown is darker, more vast, and dangerous than we can ever comprehend. The term "release the Kraken" became popular thanks to the 1981 fantasy film *Clash of the Titans*, in which Greek god Poseidon releases his Kraken in order to destroy the king of Argos, Acrisius. Poseidon is willing to do pretty much anything to defeat Acrisius; he'd even release a monster with the potential to destroy the world. Is Takeda as determined as Poseidon?

Victoria attributes "flowers are the earth's way of laughing" to Dominik, but, like his art and his women, he stole this quote from someone more renowned than he: poet and essayist Ralph Waldo Emerson (1803–1882).

WHO'S THAT GUY? Before he was charming the pants off Victoria, James Purefoy (Dominik Wright) was wooing another powerful and headstrong woman: Cleopatra. The British actor is best known stateside for his portrayal of Mark Antony in the HBO series *Rome* (2005–2007). He currently stars in Fox's *The Following* as a charismatic serial killer opposite Kevin Bacon's FBI agent. Across the pond, he's a respected theater actor, having starred in productions such as *King Lear*, *Hamlet*, and *Death of a Salesman*.

BORROWED FROM THE BOOK Victoria's obsessive devotion to Daniel mirrors Madame de Villefort's relationship with her son, Édouard. Both are second wives with something to prove, and their sons are the one legitimate connection they have to the world of privilege. Both women resort to crime, with Victoria paying to have Daniel beaten and Madame de Villefort trying to kill her stepdaughter, Valentine, to ensure her son receives a full inheritance.

BEHIND THE SCENES You might think that having your son beat up in order to get him out of prison is taking things too far, but Madeleine Stowe doesn't. Victoria will do whatever it takes to protect Daniel, and Stowe — a mother herself — understands and respects that. "I feel it is absolutely justified," she said at the *Revenge* Paleyfest panel.

REVENGENDA When did Declan get so smart? Does Victoria have a plan for this affair she's having? What is going to happen to Charlotte now that she feels everyone has betrayed her? What will Mason Treadwell write next? Why did Emily make that key imprint?

REVENGESPIRATION
"Whatever, or whomever you're doing, you'd better damn well be discreet about it." — Conrad Grayson

ALFRED HITCHCOCK
AND *REVENGE*

∞∞∞∞∞∞∞∞∞∞∞∞∞∞∞∞∞∞∞∞∞∞∞∞∞∞∞∞∞∞∞∞

Mike Kelley borrows many elements from Alfred Hitchcock for *Revenge*, right down to his two main characters: Emily Thorne and Victoria Grayson.

Hitchcock frequently cast blondes in his films for characters who seem icy and aloof but are actually extremely emotional, and occasionally even criminal. Grace Kelly, the embodiment of this archetype, starred in many of Hitchcock's films and she's a point of reference for Emily Thorne for the entire *Revenge* team — from Mike Kelley to the wardrobe department to Emily VanCamp.

Hitchcock's films also frequently feature domineering, meddling mothers and their fraught relationships with their children. The difficult mothers in *Rope, Notorious, Psycho, Shadow of a Doubt* and *The Birds* make Victoria Grayson look downright angelic.

But that's just the beginning of the Hitchcock influence on *Revenge*. Kelley employs many of the filmmaker's signature devices and subjects, including the use of likable and charming sociopaths (Emily Thorne), ordinary people being brought into extraordinary circumstances (David Clarke being framed, Nolan becoming a friend-in-revenge), brandy (Conrad's drink of choice), murder (Frank, Tyler, Roger Halsted, and David Clarke), falls from high buildings (Lydia's five-story crash), mistaken identity (Emily and Amanda swapping lives, Tyler being mistaken for Daniel at the engagement party), birds (a bird plays a key role in the finale), and even tennis (Daniel, Tyler, Emily, and Ashley play doubles).

To watch *Revenge* is to witness the legacy of one of the world's greatest filmmakers. To better understand

Hitchcock's impact on *Revenge*, check out the eight films below:

***Shadow of a Doubt* (1943):** When a teenager's uncle (both named Charlie) returns to town acting strangely, she suspects he's the serial killer the local police have been trying to catch. Her uncle eventually confirms her suspicions, but being a loyal relative, she chooses to keep this revelation a secret — a choice Daniel is faced with. The relationship between the teenager and the uncle is reminiscent of Emily's relationship with Fauxmanda. The teenager originally idolizes her uncle and there's an uncomfortable bond between the two of them. As she grows older, she no longer trusts her uncle, just as Fauxmanda becomes increasingly distrustful of Emily. The elder Charlie even tries to kill the younger Charlie in an effort to keep the authorities off his trail — not unlike how Emily is keen to run Fauxmanda out of town to protect her plan. One of Hitchcock's early American films, *Shadow of a Doubt* employs suspense, family drama, and the murky distinction between right and wrong that would come to define his later masterpieces.

***Rope* (1948):** Two affluent young men try to commit the perfect murder. After they commit the crime, they invite the friends and family of their victim over for a dinner party. The two men descend into paranoia as they fear their crime will be discovered, and this increasing paranoia is echoed in Tyler, Victoria, Emily, and Daniel at different points in *Revenge*. And everything falls apart at the party, something that happens all the time in the Hamptons.

***Strangers on a Train* (1951):** Two strangers, Guy and Bruno, meet — you guessed it! — on a train. Bruno believes they've agreed to each murder someone in the other's life. Guy doesn't. After Bruno commits murder, he grows angry with Guy for not living up to his end of the bargain and takes extreme measures. Like Emily and Fauxmanda, Guy and Bruno have an intense and vaguely sexual relationship. Emily, like Bruno, is determined to the point of being deranged and Guy, like Fauxmanda, is weak. Guilt, loyalty, and emotional manipulation feature heavily in this adaptation of the Patricia Highsmith novel, just as they do on *Revenge*.

Rear Window (1954): A photographer with a broken leg passes the time while recovering watching his neighbors through his back window. He becomes convinced that one of them murdered his wife. Hitchcock's neighborly surveillance is echoed in Victoria's constant watch over Emily's beach house and her obsession with the idea that not everything is as it seems next door, and when he's stuck at home under house arrest in Daniel's obsessive monitoring of Emily's front door because he's convinced she has feelings for Jack. In *Rear Window*, the photographer's theory is proven correct, just as Victoria and Daniel are right about Emily.

Vertigo (1958): Considered by many to be one of Hitchcock's defining films, *Vertigo* follows retired police detective Scottie Ferguson as he tracks a friend's wife, Madeleine Elster. After Madeleine apparently commits suicide, Scottie becomes obsessed with her and transforms his new love interest, Judy Barton, into the likeness of the deceased woman. Jack and Fauxmanda's relationship is reminiscent of the relationship between the police detective and the new girlfriend. Jack so badly wants her to be Amanda Clarke that he gives her memories and attributes that she doesn't actually have, ignores the parts of her story that don't make sense, and, when she disappears, obsessively stalks her.

North by Northwest (1959): Roger O. Thornhill is mistaken for a murderer and spends much of the film on the run. To remain free, he must do morally questionable things, just as Emily and Victoria do to protect their liberty. *North by Northwest* is considered to be Hitchcock's most stylish film. This sense of style, along with the movie's themes of deception, confusion, and moral ambiguity are mimicked by *Revenge*.

Psycho (1960): In a crazed moment, secretary Marion Crane steals from her company. Before she meets her lover, she's brutally murdered at the Bates Motel. Norman Bates, like Emily, lacks what Hitchcock believed people need in order to be happy: love, family, and home. When watching *Psycho*, pay particular attention to the score and how it's used to build suspense. Composed by Bernard Herrmann, a frequent Hitchcock collaborator, *Psycho*'s score has influenced many film and TV scores, including *Revenge*'s.

Marnie (1964): Marnie is a charismatic young woman who happens to be a liar and a thief. When widower Mark Rutland falls in love with her, their relationship is extremely difficult, thanks to Marnie's psychological problems. Like in the relationships between Jack and Fauxmanda, Daniel and Emily, and Conrad and Victoria, Marnie's history and tendency to lie complicates things. Hitchcock used painted backgrounds for the film, emphasizing the surreal nature of Marnie's world. *Revenge* uses green-screened backgrounds to achieve a similarly unsettling effect.

"Justice, like beauty, is in the eye of the beholder. Some see an innocent victim, others see evil incarnate getting exactly what's deserved."

1.18 JUSTICE

AIRED April 25, 2012
WRITTEN BY Sallie Patrick and Liz Tigelaar
DIRECTED BY Bobby Roth

Daniel Grayson's trial is one for the ages, and everyone is angling for the verdict they want.

"Justice" opens up four months in the future, with Daniel's trial well under way. Very little progress has been made: the Graysons have yet to find another fall guy for Tyler's murder and Jack is still chasing Fauxmanda all over the east coast. However, everyone is still struggling to answer the same question: what is just and what is going too far? Is Emily justified in taking down the Graysons to avenge her father? Were the Graysons justified in destroying David Clarke to protect their family? When does the end justify the means?

This is the question Victoria and Conrad have been grappling with since the David Clarke trial of 1995. They protected their lifestyle and their children, but at what cost? Their very privileged existence is, in part, to blame for why Daniel is in this current mess. Tyler wanted Daniel's life. Emily (in Victoria's eyes) wants Daniel's name and money. And now the Occupy movement and its supporters want to see the 1% get what's coming to them. Daniel may be innocent of murder, but he's guilty of abusing his privilege. He escaped punishment after nearly ending the life of his cocktail-waitress girlfriend last summer but, until now, he never had to take the justice system seriously.

Declan is trying to take advantage of the justice system as well. Lying

on the stand is wrong. But he can justify doing so if it means protecting his brother, a good-hearted man trying to do what is right at the risk of being taken down by the Grayson machine. The battle of Declan versus the Graysons is, in a small way, representative of the Occupy movement: a little guy doing what he can to attack those who have gotten away with murder (both figuratively and literally in the Graysons' case). He's making the Graysons ask themselves why they are being targeted and what they can do about it. Declan's small, young, and scared, but he's standing up and doing what he believes is right — just as any protester would.

Daniel's trial is the Graysons' worst nightmare, forcing them to face their demons. Their shady behavior has caught up with them again in a replication of the trial that has shaped their lives for the past two decades. This one-two punch eats Victoria alive, causing her to question her choices, but it gives Conrad the confidence to aggressively guard what's left of his family's reputation, especially when it means eliminating Dominik and ending Victoria's relationship with him, which was the only thing making her happy.

For the first time, Victoria prioritizes her conscience and her feelings over her money and her power. After years of privileging Grayson interests over her own, and being consumed by guilt and loneliness, she's trying to right those wrongs — and right what she did to David Clarke — by following her heart. For Victoria, the ends no longer justify the means.

BEST SERVED COLD Conrad served it up in "Justice," taking out Victoria's lover and cleaning up her mess in the span of the afternoon. As Victoria slowly but surely falls apart, it's becoming evident who the real backbone of the Grayson family is: Conrad.

HAMPTONS HOMAGE The episode opens with Emily quoting Clarence Darrow, one of the greatest American defense lawyers of all time. He first earned his reputation when, as a law student in 1924, he defended Nathan Freudenthal Leopold Jr. and Richard Albert Loeb, two wealthy University of Chicago students charged with the murder of 14-year-old

Bobby Franks. Called the "trial of the century," it garnered substantial media attention across the country. America watched intently and wondered why two young men with the world at their feet would commit such a heinous crime. The Daniel Grayson trial is the 21st-century equivalent of Leopold and Loeb: a young man who has it all decides to commit murder just because he can. The difference is that Leopold and Loeb were found guilty, and we know Daniel is innocent of murder.

Mini-Frank's name is Lee Moran. Lee shares a last name with Patrick Moran, the head of ABC's drama department and the person responsible for giving the production team behind *Revenge*, Marty Bowen and Wyck Godfrey, a TV deal.

Nolan calls Emily "Countess," which is the most direct dialogue reference to *The Count of Monte Cristo* in *Revenge* yet.

WHO'S THAT GUY? Robbie Amell (Adam Connor) has built his career playing boyfriends. The Canadian actor played Casey Macdonald's boyfriend Max on the Nickelodeon series *Life with Derek* (2006–2008), a boyfriend in the Ashley Tisdale project *Picture This* (2008), Robin Scherbatzky's puppy-like boyfriend, Scooby, in two episodes of *How I Met Your Mother* (2011), and True Jackson's love interest and eventual boyfriend Jimmy in *True Jackson, VP* (2008–2011). *Special bonus trivia:* In *True Jackson, VP*, Amell's character was in a band called Fire and Ice.

BORROWED FROM THE BOOK As a result of the Count's meddling, Fernand's criminal activity is uncovered and investigated by the court. A long trial ensues, and Fernand is found guilty. Fernand's trial tears his family apart and reveals where true alliances lie, which is what Daniel's trial does to the Graysons.

Albert keeps a portrait of his mother in his home. In the portrait, his mother is mournful, hopeful, and contemplative, just like Victoria in Dominik's portrait of her. These portraits reflect the decisions these two women have made in life and love and the consequences they've faced as a result.

Just as Conrad puts an end to Victoria and Dominik's affair, Baron Danglars ends his wife's affair with the man who gave her insider information about the market. As long as his wife's affair helps Danglars, he tolerates her indiscretion. But as soon as it has the potential to hurt him, his family, or his money, he wants it over. Danglars, like Conrad, follows his wife closely and knows about every affair — even those that predate their marriage.

BEHIND THE SCENES Why is it that some characters like Tyler Barrol and Lydia Davis keep coming back, but others, like Grandpa Grayson and Dominik Wright, are written out in only a few episodes? Whenever a new character is brought into the *Revenge* world, it is done with "a long-term, a mid-term, and a short-term plan," Mike Kelley told *TV Line*. From there, how long they stay depends on a variety of factors: "It often has to do with the chemistry of who gets cast and who fits in this world." Kelley admitted (without naming names!) that some guest stars didn't quite work out, but others — like Ashton Holmes and Margarita Levieva — worked out better than planned. The actors, like the characters they play, are full of surprises, and Kelley tries to create space in the storylines for the unexpected to happen.

REVENGENDA Is Mason still kicking around, writing his blog? How did Emily not know the Graysons killed her father? Will Charlotte ever forgive Declan for lying on the stand? Now that the charges against Daniel have been dropped, where do he and Emily stand?

REVENGESPIRATION
"All you have to do is tell the truth." — Charlotte Grayson

REVENGE READING
EURIPIDES' *MEDEA*

Medea is a tragic figure in Greek mythology, and possibly one of the earliest representations of revenge in Western culture. Euripides' 431 BC play is based on the many stories about Medea passed down through generations before him. Medea is the wife of Jason, the ancient Greek hero. Or, rather, *was* the wife of Jason. After he abandons her to marry the daughter of the king of Creon in order to better his social status, Medea decides to seek revenge on her ex-husband by murdering his new family. After she kills his new wife and her father, the king, Medea decides that death is an insufficient punishment for Jason and murders his sons — her own children. The plan works: Jason is devastated and his life is destroyed. But Medea is left with nothing too.

Victoria has a "Medea complex," a term used to describe a woman who harms (or kills) her children. Like Medea, Victoria uses her children as pawns to get back at or influence her husband. Victoria believes when she hurts her children — she emotionally manipulates them, she slaps them, and she pays to have Daniel beaten in jail — she's doing it for a greater good. But all she's really doing is harming her children and further alienating herself from her family.

While Emily first balks at the thought of involving innocent people in her plan, this resolve wavers as she becomes more determined, following the same evolution as Medea. Emily becomes more and more like Medea with each step. She outs Nolan as Tyler's lover in order to get back at Tyler. She plans to out Charlotte as David Clarke's daughter to get back at Victoria. Finally, she chooses to frame Lee Moran, a petty thug who is in over his head but is (relatively) harmless, for Tyler's murder by planting the blood-soaked hoodie in his car.

Medea succeeds in her quest to destroy Jason's life, but only at the expense of destroying her own as well. If Victoria and Emily continue to harm those who consider her family, will they suffer the same fate?

• ● •

"If the people I've come to bring justice to cannot be bound with a quest for absolution than neither will I."

1.19 ABSOLUTION

AIRED May 2, 2012
WRITTEN BY Nikki Toscano and Ryan Scott
DIRECTED BY Sanford Bookstaver

Now that Daniel is a free man, he makes some big decisions and Emily makes a big discovery.

There are two kinds of families: those you are born into and those you choose. Sometimes these two peacefully coexist; other times, you have to choose between them.

Throughout the season, Nolan has helped Emily and the Porters, the members of his adopted family, and in "Absolution," we find out why. He owes everything to his aunt Carole and her generosity. Nolan is a fan of paying it forward. Jack and Declan are struggling, emotionally and financially, as they try to keep up with the Graysons, keep their bar afloat, and keep Declan in school. Like David and Carole did for him, Nolan offers the Porters the support they need. Nolan's dream was to build communications technology and Emily's plan is to destroy a family's well-being, but both began as social misfits with an idea and the drive to realize it. Like David and Carole, Nolan's chosen to believe in someone else's crazy vision.

So has Daniel. He learns his family's dark secrets and decides to align himself fully with his father and with the Grayson name. While this feels like a complete 180 from the poetry-quoting, Paris-dreaming Daniel, it's a development that makes sense. Daniel has always demanded honesty and promised it to his loved ones. Conrad gives him the truth, entrusting him with knowledge in a sign of respect and equal standing. Daniel now understands there are burdens that come with being a Grayson just as there are privileges. Conrad spins his story as the actions of a patriarch protecting his family, and Daniel, keen to be a man who fights for things bigger than himself, responds to that. He sees Conrad's crimes as sins committed in the name of family, while his mother's are sins of self-interest.

Daniel's support gives Conrad renewed strength. Like Victoria, Conrad's tired of the lies and covering his tracks. As long as Victoria is around, longing for David and full of regret, Conrad can't move on. He needs Victoria out of his life; as she listens to her conscience rather than her greedy instincts, she becomes a viable threat to Conrad, his company, and the Grayson legacy.

As Conrad finds renewed strength in Daniel, Victoria finds it in Charlotte. With Dominik gone and Daniel gone rogue, Charlotte is Victoria's last hope for a relationship built on love and understanding. Victoria begins to face what she did to David Clarke, and part of that is addressing the reality that Charlotte is his daughter. In a way, Victoria wants to make a new family, even if that means destroying herself in the process of clearing David's name.

Just as there is absolution in acceptance, there's absolution in confession. We see both Conrad and Victoria trying this: Victoria confesses her feelings about David Clarke to Charlotte and Conrad confesses what he did to David Clarke to Daniel. These confessions give Victoria and Conrad both a sense of freedom and acceptance they've been searching for and bring them closer to their children. It seems the Grayson parents are finally learning that you can't build a long-lasting, respectful relationship on lies and deceit. You can only build it on truth and respect. By offering these olive branches to Daniel and Charlotte, their family is simultaneously closer than ever and on the edge of disaster.

For the Graysons, it seems that absolution can emerge only from destruction. Whether it's the destruction of those who did wrong (as Victoria is trying to destroy Conrad), those who don't matter (as Conrad destroyed Dominik's career), or of the self (as Charlotte and Victoria are doing), the Graysons are on their way to destroying everything they've ever worked for. But maybe that's the only way Victoria, Conrad, Daniel, and Charlotte will ever be free.

BEST SERVED COLD Daniel shows that cold blood is a genetic trait when he declares his allegiance to his father on national television, crushing Emily's and Victoria's hopes for him.

WHO'S THAT GUY? In 1987, Tess Harper (Carole Miller) was nominated for an Academy Award for Best Supporting Actress for her role in *Crimes of the Heart* (1986). While she didn't win, it launched a successful movie career with parts in films like *Ishtar* (1987), *The Man in the Moon* (1991), *The Jackal* (1997), and *No Country for Old Men* (2007). Recently, Harper has been spending time on television. Her notable TV roles include *Early Edition* (1998–2000), where she played Gary Hobson's mom — opposite fellow *Revenge* guest star William Devane, who played Gary's dad — and *Breaking Bad* (2008–2010), where she played Jesse Pinkman's mom.

BORROWED FROM THE BOOK After his father is found guilty, Albert decides he must do all that he can to avenge him and challenges the Count of Monte Cristo to a duel. This is the same reaction Daniel has to the "witch hunt" against his father. The difference is that Daniel is aware of his father's crimes while Albert believes in his father's innocence. Similarly, the Morrels always believed in Dantès' innocence, just like Carole Miller believed that David Clarke was not the monster he was set up to look like.

BEHIND THE SCENES When Mike Kelley offered James Morrison a role on *Revenge,* the veteran actor jumped at the chance — even though he had no idea what role he'd play. At the time, all Kelley knew was that the character would be called "The Bearded Man" (which, as we know, was later changed to "The White-Haired Man"). So why did Morrison say yes? "[Kelley] promised me that I'd be the most evil bad guy of all time," Morrison told entertainment website *Geno's World,* "and I was in!"

Cynthia McFadden is often asked to make guest appearances in films and on television, but usually turns them down. But the ABC News correspondent was keen to interview Daniel Grayson. Early in her career, she covered a real-life murder in the Hamptons. McFadden had one request before stepping on set: that she would get to consult on her script. It's a good thing she did — she found two factual errors in her lines!

REVENGENDA Who is the White-Haired Man? How does he know Conrad? What's Daniel's next move? Now that Daniel is a true Grayson, what will Emily do to him?

REVENGESPIRATION
"When I choose to react, you'll know it." — Victoria Grayson

REVENGE READING
EDWARD ALBEE'S
WHO'S AFRAID OF VIRGINIA WOOLF?

At the *Revenge* Paleyfest panel, Henry Czerny compared Conrad and Victoria's relationship to George and Martha's in the 1962 Edward Albee play *Who's Afraid of Virginia Woolf?* It's an apt comparison. In fact, Conrad and Victoria might even be worse than George and Martha.

Who's Afraid of Virginia Woolf? takes place in the span of a single evening. George and Martha, a bitter middle-aged couple, are entertaining a young professor, Nick, who's new to the university where George works and where Martha's father is president. Nick, and his wife, Honey, become unwitting pawns in the battle of Martha versus George. As the night progresses, we learn just how damaged George and Martha's relationship is, as they both tear into the most private aspects of their lives in order to hurt each other and impress upon their guests just how awful the other is.

George and Martha represent a possible future for Nick and Honey, one where the promises of young love and a budding career go unfulfilled. Small problems can become huge when they are left to fester, and George and Martha's marriage gets worse because they are unable to communicate with each other in an open and honest way. Victoria and Conrad face the same problem: instead of addressing problems head-on and discussing their feelings freely, they behave as opponents in a game of one-upping each other. This, in turn, only creates more distance between them and more problems.

Within the play, Albee uses George and Martha's interactions with Nick, Honey, and the audience to explore the differences between how a marriage presents itself in public and how it functions in private. On the surface, George and Martha seem to have it all. They are a powerful couple in the university and George has a successful career. But they are extremely dissatisfied with their lives and with each other. Like George and Martha, Conrad and Victoria went through great lengths to create the public perception of a happy marriage: they had a *New York Times* profile written about their successful 25 years together and choose to present a united front through Daniel's trial. But, like George and Martha, this is all a façade. They are so unhappy that they find pleasure only in tearing each other down and attacking others.

By the end of the play, George and Martha have beaten each other up so badly, they have nowhere to go but up. They are literary proof that a marriage is truly a partnership; the engaged parties can build it up or destroy it. Conrad and Victoria seem set on destroying each other, just like George and Martha. But at what cost?

• ● •

"One way or another, these people are going to pay. They're going to pay for what they did."

1.20 LEGACY

AIRED May 9, 2012
WRITTEN BY Dan Dworkin and Jay Beattie
DIRECTED BY Eric Laneuville

It's 2002. Emily Thorne is still Amanda Clarke and decides to find out what really happened to her father and who is to blame for it.

In 2011, the David Clarke conspiracy was almost 20 years old. In "Legacy," *Revenge* heads to the past, offering viewers insight into what's going on in the present — and into what might happen in the future.

In 2002, Amanda Clarke is angry. Even before she learns the truth about what happened to her father, she's aggressive and always up for a fight. Meeting the raging 18-year-old Amanda shows us two things: that she was always someone looking for a battle and how much she's managed to internalize her anger — and her guilt about not believing her father was innocent — in order to unleash a life-altering, all-consuming plan to take down the people who destroyed her father.

Nolan has a goal of his own: to do right by those he's made promises to or those he's wronged. This was already apparent in 2011, but 2002 shows just how desperate he is to make things right for Amanda. He's equally determined to make things right with the Porters, who he inadvertently made homeless. Nolan doesn't want to be alone in his belief that David Clarke was a good guy, and he wants others to believe the same of him — that he's not an arrogant billionaire like Jack believes the man who bought his home is. Still dealing with the fall-out of his own family, Nolan has the opportunity to put two broken families back together again. If he can fix Amanda's memories of her father and keep the secret about the Porters' mother, it means he's done more for both these families than anyone has ever done for his.

Jack has the same goal as Nolan: to keep his family together. It's why he moves back into the bar with his dad, why he's angry about his dad selling their home, why he's so upset by the New Year's kiss between his girlfriend and Nolan, and why he believes Montauk isn't so bad. He's quick to act out against anyone — or anything — that gets in his way of maintaining the status quo at the Stowaway. By 2011, Jack's calmed down, but he has this same goal — and same fighting spirit. He's just better at internalizing it and worn down after years of struggling to keep his family afloat.

2002 shows us just how opportunistic Lydia Davis and Mason Treadwell have always been. They both originally participated in the conspiracy because of the advantages it gave them, and 10 years later, both are still looking to capitalize on what they did: Lydia by using it to hook up with the man she's loved for a decade and Mason by having a little fun at the Graysons' expense and possibly dredging up new material for his work. Lydia and Mason provide a stark contrast to Roger Halsted. The disgraced and depressed accountant has paid for his betrayal with a decade-long internal battle. The only thing that Roger wants is to be free of the guilt and torment, so he chooses to help Emily. His reward is to be relieved of his pain — through the most extreme measure possible.

Lydia and Mason of 2002 represent one possible future for those involved in the David Clark conspiracy; Roger represents the other. Lydia and Mason are looking over their shoulders, but also keeping an eye on their future: what or whom can they take advantage of next? They refuse to accept any responsibility or feel any remorse about what they did to David Clarke and his daughter. Roger, on the other hand, became consumed by the past.

In 2002, Victoria and Conrad are standing at a crossroads: Conrad is eager to let go of David Clarke's house and move on, just as Lydia and Mason have. But Victoria is reviled by the thought of spending more time with "those people" and can't let go. She keeps an empty beach house in order to revisit the past. Their party was rich with tension: as they continue to travel down different paths, their marriage seems doomed (as we know it is).

Between 2002 and 2011, each character has internalized something, whether it is anger (Emily and Jack), guilt (Emily, Victoria, and Nolan), feelings for someone else (Lydia, Victoria, and Frank) or fear (Mason and Victoria). As we move back into the present and they ring in 2012, what matters is not what they did, it's how they deal with it — and what might happen when they just can't take it anymore.

BEST SERVED COLD Emily shows her angry and violent streak at the club when she bashes a random guy's head in because he decided to hook up with someone else. She's ready and willing to fight almost anyone.

HAMPTONS HOMAGE When Jack's girlfriend, Kyla, mentions that Montauk in winter is like *The Shining*, she likely doesn't realize how apt her words are. The tourist town in Stephen King's 1977 horror novel is as deserted as Montauk when the snow comes, making both settings extra spooky. *The Shining* is about a hotel that has the power to psychologically control its inhabitants, which is, in a way, weirdly reminiscent of David Clarke's beach house. Bad things happen in both places, which hold strong emotional resonances. The beach house has a hold on Victoria's mind, propelling her to keep it and mourn for David rather than move on. It also has a hold on Emily; it's not only a fond childhood memory, but it's where she learns the truth about her father, decides to avenge his name, and serves as the headquarters for her revenge plan.

Conrad has Monte Cristo cigars for his 1992 New Year's Eve party to smoke with David and Bill, and the Graysons have Monte Cristo sandwiches up for grabs on their buffet, a delicious concoction of ham and cheese.

WHO'S THAT GUY? John Billingsley (Roger Halsted) is best known to TV fans as Dr. Phlox on *Star Trek: Enterprise* (2001–2005). But Billingsley hasn't slowed down since the *Enterprise* completed its final voyage. His TV work includes *Prison Break* (2006), *CSI* (2007), *Grey's Anatomy* (2007), *24* (2009), *Criminal Minds* (2009), and a recurring role as coroner Mike Spencer on *True Blood* (2008–2012). His stint on *Cold Case* (2004–2005) as serial killer George Marks is especially notable: he's the only murderer on the show who ever got away with it. *Special bonus trivia:* Billingsley guest-starred as himself on *Roswell* (2001), the last major TV series Nick Wechsler worked on.

BORROWED FROM THE BOOK It's clear at the Grayson's 1992 New Year's Eve party that everyone at Grayson Global likes and respects David Clarke. When we first meet Dantès in *The Count of Monte Cristo*, he has the same ease with those he works with. He's respected, trusted, and genuinely liked by all — and that's why he was such a desirable target for his enemies.

Dantès declares the moment he discovers the treasure to be both "joyous and terrible," because it is at that moment he knows what he must do. The similar defining moment for Emily is when she reads her father's journals. It is a joyous moment to discover the truth about her father and establish a connection with him, but it's also a terrible moment because now that she knows the truth, she feels obligated to do something about it.

The Morrels struggle financially and have a lot of debt. Their once-prosperous shipping company is in near ruins. They count on their ship, the *Pharaon*, to come to port so Monsieur Morrel can pay his creditors. Dantès steps in, anonymously, to ensure that the family doesn't fall into ruin. While the Porters own a bar, and it's Mr. Porter's wife who comes calling for cash, the premise is the same: they can't pay the debts they owe, but thanks to a wealthy man, Nolan, Carl Porter manages to keep his livelihood and dignity.

BEHIND THE SCENES Whatever you do, don't call "Legacy" a flashback episode. According to Mike Kelley, it's an episode from 2002, "one from the *Revenge* archives." Kelley and his team had a lot of fun imagining what the characters were like 10 years ago and hoped fans would too. "It's a bit of a love letter to fans."

REVENGENDA After Emily decided on her fate, how did she set her plan in motion? Will Jack's nosy girlfriend resurface in the present day? When do Victoria and David start getting it on? Did David and Amanda come over for brunch on New Year's Day?

REVENGESPIRATION
"It's perverse, don't you think? Destroy the man you love then weep for him eternally?" — Conrad Grayson

REVENGE READING
AGATHA CHRISTIE'S
AND THEN THERE WERE NONE

For Mason Treadwell, the Graysons' party felt like a reprise of Agatha Christie's *And Then There Were None* (also known as *Ten Little Indians*). In the 1939 novel — which is the bestselling mystery of all time — 10 strangers are invited to a party at a mansion on a remote island. It is soon revealed they've been summoned to the island to meet their own end, one by one.

In *And Then There Were None*, Christie examines the

relationship between responsibility and guilt. Each party guest played a different role in a death of someone they knew and feels varying degrees of guilt, which don't necessarily correlate to the level of responsibility. The same can be said for the partygoers in *Revenge*. Roger Halsted is arguably less responsible for what happened to David Clarke than the Graysons, but he feels extremely guilty, and he pays the ultimate price. Lydia, on the other hand, was more involved. She lied on the stand, but doesn't feel guilty about it. And instead of suffering for what she did, she's continuously rewarded: getting the beach house and beginning an affair with Conrad.

And Then There Were None, like *Revenge*, explores the subjectivity of justice and the consequences of someone taking justice into her own hands. Who gets to determine what is just? Who is responsible for making sure that justice is served? Is it just for someone to murder these people because they were involved in the death of another? Who has the power to make such a decision? These big questions are left unresolved at the end of the party in *And Then There Were None*, leaving readers to draw their own conclusions about justice, morality, and responsibility, just as viewers must with *Revenge*.

• ● •

> *"For most the final stage of grief is acceptance. But for me grief is a life sentence without clemency."*

1.21 GRIEF

AIRED May 16, 2012
WRITTEN BY Mark Fish and Joe Fazzio
DIRECTED BY Randy Zisk

The upcoming wedding pushes Daniel and Emily apart, while the death of Sammy brings Jack and Emily together. Victoria becomes more determined to take Conrad down, but Daniel's allegiance to him gets in the way.

"Grief" may be the penultimate episode of *Revenge*'s first season, but thanks to Sammy's death (and heart-wrenching performances by Emily VanCamp and Nick Wechsler), it's the season's emotional climax, setting viewers up for what's sure to be an insane finale.

Sammy's death shakes up Jack and Emily, releasing a well of emotion that had been kept carefully in check. For both, Sammy represented a happier time. Jack once said that his childhood ended when he learned what happened to Amanda's family, but he finally says good-bye to it when he says good-bye to Sammy. He was Jack's last connection to his happy past. The same is true of Emily. A beloved reminder of her life before her father was taken away, Sammy's death allows Emily the space to grieve, to say good-bye to her father and her lost childhood.

All season, Emily has rejected emotional connection to keep focused on vengeance. But as she opens herself up to experience the pain of Sammy's death, she realizes it's not too late to experience human connection. In grieving with Jack, it's the first time Emily embraces her true feelings in front of someone else. It is also the first time she explores the possibility of a real relationship with someone — even if it is only for a few moments. Jack has also been holding on to a dream, tying his future and his feelings to Amanda. By saying good-bye to Sammy, he finally says good-bye to Amanda and opens himself up to new possibilities, one that includes a future with Emily.

Sammy's death also frees Emily to look toward the future: with the dog she loved gone, can she open herself up to love Jack? And if so, what does this mean for her future? Even before Sammy's death, Emily has an eye on the future unlike ever before. Her focus on finishing the Graysons is laser-like now — she compromises a simple wedding planning meeting to follow Nolan's White-Haired-Man stalking. This act shows how dedicated Emily is to her cause, but it also shows that she's running out of patience. After months of careful and patient plotting, she's ready to battle, even if her fidgety nature is making Daniel suspicious. The more Daniel becomes a Grayson, the less on the fence Emily is about her plan to take the family down. She's no longer reveling in inflicting pain on those around her. She just wants to get it done so she can move on.

Emily is not the only one itching for a fight: Daniel is ready to battle Jack, Victoria is ready to battle Conrad, Conrad is ready to battle the White-Haired Man, and Nolan is ready to battle whoever he must in order to prevent Emily from killing someone. While Conrad, Daniel, and Victoria were each unable to protect their family from the very public mess of the murder trial, they feel that by taking a stand for what they believe in now — Daniel by giving the family good PR, Conrad by settling things with the White-Haired Man, and Victoria by exposing Conrad to the SEC — they can fix their respective messes and atone.

Emily may assure Nolan that he doesn't know what she's capable of, but the real question is what everyone else involved is capable of — including the mysterious White-Haired Man — and what it all means for Emily's revengenda.

BEST SERVED COLD Victoria shreds the fake De Kooning painting, a symbol of her past with Conrad, and stings his mistress in one incredibly dramatic moment.

HAMPTONS HOMAGE Conrad calls Victoria a "demonic succubus" when she stops by his NYC apartment. A succubus is a demon who seduces

men; the man's life deteriorates after each time he sleeps with the succubus. Victoria has used her sexual power consistently throughout her life, and every man she's slept with (that we know about) has suffered: Conrad ran Dominik out of town, David Clarke was framed and murdered, and, if Victoria has her way, Conrad's company is about to crumble.

WHO'S THAT GUY? James Morrison (the White-Haired Man) is not only an accomplished stage and screen actor, he's a yoga instructor and published poet. He's best known to TV fans as counter terrorist unit director Bill Buchanan on *24* (2005–2009), but you might also recognize him as Lieutenant Colonel T.C. McQueen from *Space: Above and Beyond* (1995–1996), former practice owner William White on *Private Practice* (2009–2010), or hospital CEO John Morrissey on *Hawthorne* (2009–2011).

BORROWED FROM THE BOOK Dantès ends up imprisoned because he is caught in the crossfire of two political movements: the royalists, who want the monarchy to stay as is, and the Bonapartists, who want Napoleon in charge. In *The Count of Monte Cristo*, Dantès winds up in jail because his friends betray him, but it wouldn't have happened without a larger conspiracy trying to put Napoleon back in power in France. The same is true for David Clarke's arrest and murder: it was a small act made possible because of a conspiracy larger than the Graysons, and whose depths we are only just learning about.

BEHIND THE SCENES Mike Kelley originally intended for Sammy to die earlier in the season, but when his own dog of 14 years passed away, he couldn't bring himself to do it. When Kelley finally felt he could share the experience with others, he channeled his own emotions to write the scene. "It was very emotional for me, and really, all the things Jack was saying to Sammy were pretty much verbatim how I let my dog go," he told *Entertainment Weekly*. Kelley found the experience therapeutic. "It was something really emotional that I wanted to share with people." The end result was one of the most touching and emotional moments we've seen in the first season of *Revenge*. Someone give that dog — whose real name is Jax — an Emmy.

REVENGENDA Why did Carole help out Emily? What are Ashley, Emily, and Daniel going to do about the upcoming wedding? Will Lydia continue to support Conrad or take Victoria's immunity offer? Will Emily kill the White-Haired Man? Is Nolan still alive?

REVENGESPIRATION
"You don't know what I am or what I'm capable of." — Emily Thorne

REVENGE READING
GEORGE ORWELL'S *1984*

Emily hid her secret video camera in a (fake) biography of George Orwell. Orwell is best known for his 1949 novel *1984*, which explores the dangerous ramifications of a totalitarian society. In the world of *1984*, the Party controls the government and their leader is the all-watching, all-knowing Big Brother. Dissent is illegal and there is no such thing as secrets. Winston Smith, *1984*'s protagonist, does what he can to resist this tightly controlled and demanding regime, with protests as small as having sex and as big as writing down his anti-Party thoughts, which is one of the worst crimes a citizen can commit.

The obvious reference to *1984* in *Revenge* is that Emily and Daniel are being watched, just like the citizens of the novel. Emily also spied on Kingsly's mistress and Conrad Grayson by bugging their homes, and both Nolan and Emily watch people through the Shamu cam. In *Revenge*, anyone could be watching at any time.

This reference to Orwell and *1984* hints at something bigger than the David Clarke conspiracy as we know it, something bigger than even Conrad understands. In *1984*, the government is extremely secretive and there are many conspiracies. O'Brien, a supposed member of an anti-government group, turns out to be part of a government conspiracy to find dissenters. If allies are in fact enemies and enemies allies in *1984*, what could this signal for Emily and the Graysons? Do they have a mutual enemy after all?

1984 is also about control. Orwell writes, "Who controls the past controls the future. Who controls the present controls the past." In *Revenge*, the Graysons controlled the past, rewriting what happened with Flight 197. To control the present, they bribe, lie, and deceive as necessary to make sure the past stays written as is. But without power, the Grayson version of history could be rewritten, jeopardizing their future. Emily is the threat capable of that: if she gains control of the present, she can rewrite the past and change how the future will unfold.

THE SYMBOLS
OF *REVENGE*

Several symbols and motifs occur repeatedly in *Revenge*, reminding viewers about the story going on beneath Emily and Victoria's backhanded conversations. Below are six symbols worth watching for.

Double Infinity: The infinity symbol is a literal representation of the show's tagline, "what goes around comes around" (and is substituted for the "g" in *Revenge* on the title card). The two intersecting symbols represent the many dualities that define and shape *Revenge*, such as good and evil and forgiveness and vengeance. Double infinity is also used as a symbol of the commitment two people make to each other: whether it's David to Amanda, David to Victoria, Emily to David, Daniel to Emily, Nolan to

Emily, and so on. *Revenge* is about commitments and choosing which ones to honor and which ones to break.

Boxes: Several boxes play important roles in *Revenge*, including Emily's infinity box, Daniel's briefcase, Victoria's engagement present to Daniel and Emily, and the ring box Conrad gives to Lydia. With the opening of each of these boxes, something new becomes known. Emily's box and Daniel's briefcase each contains secrets, the details of past evils. Victoria's and Conrad's boxes each contain a promise. Boxes represent possibility and opportunity, but as we know from the story of Pandora's box, not all opportunities locked away will be positive — a box opened just might result in chaos.

Water: Dark, mysterious water opens each episode of *Revenge*, suggesting that we can never know what's happening below the surface. Emily has an affinity to the water, which is noted by Lydia and Daniel, suggesting there's more going on under Emily's skin than might first appear. It represents all the knowledge Emily and Victoria might never be able to access or understand. But water also represents an escape: Jack is determined to sail off to Haiti and start a new life. Its vastness holds promise just as it holds mystery.

Art: Victoria and Conrad have an expansive art collection; Emily is an artist and Conrad hides critical evidence in a forged painting. Art is subjective, and its presence on *Revenge* is a reminder that everything is open to interpretation. It's also a reminder to look for hidden meaning in things that might originally seem unimportant. Emily and Victoria get the upper hand on their enemies by seeing what others cannot see and using that to their advantage.

Time: *Revenge* uses flashforwards and flashbacks to fully tell Emily's story. But time is also a major symbol for *Revenge*: Emily hangs on to her father's engraved watch, Conrad gives Daniel a watch for his birthday, two New Year's Eve parties play an important role in *Revenge*'s past, and the White-Haired Man has clocks galore in his home. No matter how hard you try, time is something that can't be controlled or manipulated, and the passing of time represents all that Emily, Victoria, and the rest cannot control.

Red: It's in the title cards and the clothing. It's associated with fire and it's the color of blood, two things that crop up repeatedly in *Revenge*. Red also symbolizes many emotions — guilt, passion, anger, love, courage, and sacrifice — all of which are pivotal to the story of Emily Thorne and her quest for vengeance.

• ● •

"In every life there comes a day of reckoning. A time when unsettled scores demand their retribution and our own lies and transgressions are finally laid bare."

1.22 RECKONING

AIRED May 23, 2012
WRITTEN BY Mike Kelley and Mark B. Perry
DIRECTED BY Sanford Bookstaver

Emily meets the White-Haired Man face-to-face as Conrad and Victoria face the consequences of their involvement in the David Clarke conspiracy.

Revenge's season finale signals upcoming births but also brazenly dances with death. And it shows how essential hope is to life — and what happens when all hope is lost.

Several things die, almost die, or supposedly die in "Reckoning," both literally and figuratively: Emily and Daniel break up, Charlotte ODs on pills, Victoria and Lydia are presumed dead after boarding a plane that explodes (!), and Emily's vendetta against the Graysons comes to a close as key evidence is in the hands of the feds (maybe). Each death symbolizes the ending of a major story for each character, but there are just as many new beginnings — births, if you will — as well. Daniel and Ashley's eye sex signals a new relationship may be on the horizon, Conrad proposes to Lydia, Emily learns her mother is alive and has a whole new mission, and Fauxmanda returns with a giant pregnant belly, claiming she's carrying Jack's baby. While many of these transitions spell trouble, most offer hope for a new future.

It is hope that prevents Emily from crossing the line by committing murder. In the crucial moment, Emily has hope for a future with Jack — the kind of future her father wanted for her. But her choice to let the White-Haired Man live also gives viewers hope. It sends the episode into a tailspin and births new possibilities for season two.

When Victoria's plane goes down — taking with it the evidence that indicts the Graysons and exonerates David Clarke — Emily loses all hope. Her life's mission literally goes up in flames. One chapter that seemed to end was Emily's quest to avenge her father. But when Nolan shows up with a copy of the hard drive's data — and the news that Emily's mother is still alive — he gives Emily hope that not all is lost.

Just as Emily has a new commitment, so does Jack. He has just moved on from Fauxmanda to Emily, only to be faced with Fauxmanda's return. As someone who has always wanted to do good, protect others, and love with his whole heart, Jack now has the perfect — if unexpected — opportunity to do so by becoming a father. A pregnancy is a promise and parenthood the ultimate commitment, and Jack ends season one full of hope: to provide for a woman who has had a rough road in life and to provide his baby with a better life than his own.

Jack may have a baby on the way, but the new and more Grayson-esque personas that Daniel and Charlotte have been cultivating finally

© MP126 / MEDIAPUNCH INC.

214   best served cold

emerge from their cocoons in "Reckoning." Daniel now stands firmly on his father's side and Charlotte pulls a Victoria Grayson when she publicly shames Declan's new girlfriend. But Daniel and Charlotte wear these new skins differently: Daniel feels more comfortable and more powerful the further into the Grayson fold he moves. He has hope that the Graysons will weather the storm, as they always have. In the wake of his break-up with Emily, he's presented with someone who doesn't think that being a Grayson is a bad thing like his former fiancée does. Ashley, the morally ambiguous, ambitious social climber, would love nothing more than to be on the arm of a Grayson, and in their flicker of flirtation, we get a glimpse of a young Victoria on the make.

Charlotte, on the other hand, just wants to shed whatever is making her feel unhappy and worthless. She may want Declan and Jaime to suffer for hurting her, but in the end, she hurts herself. Despite their differences, as long as her mother was around, she had an example to follow, someone to emulate and strive to be like. Victoria survived much worse than Charlotte, knew how to make people pay, and keep an eye to the future. But with Victoria gone, Charlotte feels as though she's left with nothing: no father, no mother, and no boyfriend. Aimless and alone, Charlotte thinks she has nothing to live or hope for.

Which brings us to Victoria. She's hopeful that justice will prevail and David Clarke will be exonerated. She knew she was walking onto an exploding plane; Conrad told her as much. But by embracing her possible death, she's giving birth to a new future: one where she's finally free of her own guilt. So, if she was really on that plane when it exploded, she's most certainly paid the ultimate price for her wrongdoings. And if she wasn't, it's a whole new ball game.

Revenge served up a solid season of soap and suspense, and it is at its best in "'Reckoning." In the very beginning of the pilot, Confucius's wisdom teaches us to dig two graves. But if "Reckoning" is any indication of what's to come, we're going to need to dig a whole lot more.

BEST SERVED COLD Victoria gave Emily and Daniel a box of nothing for their engagement! Not only is that the bitchiest (and best!) engagement present ever, it's also the most confident. Even as she's trying to do the right thing and be a better person, she can't help but take one last icy jab at the thorn that was in her side all summer.

HAMPTONS HOMAGE The episode opens with an extreme close-up of Emily's eye, a patent move from another ABC show, *Lost*. In many ways, *Revenge* is the successor to *Lost*, which ran on ABC from 2004 to 2010. Both have single-word, heavy-handed titles that clearly define what the show is about. Both are complex cult hits with rabid fan bases. Both begin with a mysterious plane crash that changes the lives of all the characters connected to it. Both rely heavily on flashbacks (and flashforwards) to reveal more about their characters and their motives. While *Revenge* began as a soapy procedural, it quickly evolved into a complex character-driven story about more than a girl seeking revenge just as *Lost* is a complex character-driven story about so much more than surviving a plane crash. Not only is this shot of Emily's eye a powerful visual tool, it signals to viewers that *Revenge* understands the role it's filling for television fans, a responsibility it won't take lightly. So get those crazy conspiracy theories ready.

When Emily demands to be taken to Nolan Ross, the White-Haired Man says, "As you wish," a famed phrase from William Goldman's 1973 fantasy novel *The Princess Bride* and its successful 1987 film adaptation. "As you wish" is uttered by farmhand Westley whenever the lady of the house and his eventual ladylove Buttercup gives him a chore to do. It's also the phrase Westley uses to signal to Buttercup he was the Man in Black — just before she pushes him off a cliff, believing he is someone else. But the strongest reference to *The Princess Bride* comes from Emily, when she tells the White-Haired Man, "Amanda Clarke. You murdered my father. We have unfinished business," which references the infamous *Princess Bride* line, "Hello. My name is Inigo Montoya. You killed my father. Prepare to die," which were repeatedly uttered by Inigo Montoya as he prepared to avenge his father's death. And if that's not enough *The Princess Bride* goodness, Emily and the White-Haired Man both don black throughout the entire episode (at least until their big fight is over).

WHO'S THAT GUY? Michael Reilly Burke, who plays Agent John McGowen on *Revenge,* is a frequent guest star on television. His credits include *Cold Case* (2003), *The O.C.* (2004), *The West Wing* (2005), *Heroes* (2006), *24* (2007), *ER* (2009), and *Private Practice* (2010). His most notable role was playing Ted Bundy in the 2002 biopic *Ted Bundy. Special bonus trivia:* One of Burke's early TV guest spots was a six-episode string on *Providence* in 1999, which was the very first show Mike Kelley worked on.

BORROWED FROM THE BOOK In the end, Dantès doesn't end up with Mercédès, his one true love. It appears that Mike Kelley plans to keep Emily and Jack apart too, and if he stays true to the book, he may just keep them apart forever. Victoria follows in Mercédès' footsteps when she decides she'd rather be poor and alone but free of shame than continue to live a lie. Mercédès reveals her husband's wrongdoings in order to save Dantès' life, just as Victoria is willing to reveal her husband's wrongdoings in order to avenge David. Mercédès accepts the fate her choices have brought her, and only hopes for a better life for her children, as does Victoria. Mercédès and Victoria suffer most of all, even though others have far, far more to be accountable for.

Valentine is poisoned by brucine and left for dead. She only survives because her grandfather had been secretly giving her small doses to build up her immunity to the poison, suspecting she would be the next victim of poisoning. While Charlotte's own unconscious state is self-inflicted, she's teetering between life and death, just as Valentine did.

BEHIND THE SCENES Are you upset that Victoria could be dead? Madeleine Stowe isn't. Instead, she's proud that *Revenge* ended its freshman season with this bold move. "Always go for the creatively strong choice, and whether I return or not is sort of immaterial for me," Stowe told *Access Hollywood.* The original plan was for the audience to just see Victoria's car drive up to the tarmac, but Stowe and Mike Kelley felt that didn't leave enough of an impact. With Stowe's encouragement, Kelley opted for the less ambiguous but way more dramatic slow-motion walk up to the plane instead. "I think, at least for that season's end, that's a wonderful, wonderful way to go."

REVENGENDA Is Lydia dead? Is Victoria dead? Is Charlotte dead? Are Daniel and Ashley going to get together? Why didn't the White-Haired Man tell Conrad about Amanda Clarke? Why didn't he hunt her down right away? Why did he wink at Emily through the photo cam? Is Conrad still going to leave the country? Is Amanda really pregnant with Jack's baby? Where is Emily's mom? How does the White-Haired Man know Emily's mom? What is Emily going to do now?

REVENGESPIRATION
"Let it play." — Emily Thorne

REVENGE READING
FRANK MILLER'S *BATMAN: YEAR ONE*

Nolan may call Emily "Batgirl," but she's actually more like Batgirl's mentor, Batman. Batman was first introduced in 1939 and is one of DC Comics' most successful superheroes. Batman is the alter ego of Bruce Wayne, a billionaire who trained himself to fight crime after his parents were murdered. He vows to bring as many criminals as he can to justice to avenge the death of his parents. Like Emily, Bruce is really, really rich but doesn't have any superpowers. Instead he uses intellect, technology, wealth, and martial arts training to take out his enemies. Like Emily, Bruce spent several years abroad honing his skills. Like Emily, Bruce is always a step or two ahead of those he is trying to take down, but he has one important rule: he doesn't kill.

Batman has many storylines from comics, films, and TV incarnations, but the one most relevant to *Revenge* is the 1987 origin story, *Batman: Year One*. This comic chronicles the first year after Bruce Wayne returns to Gotham after 12 years abroad. Bruce's origin story is twinned with the origin story of Lieutenant James Gordon, the only honest cop in a sea of corruption. As the story progresses, they realize just how much they need each other.

Wayne and Gordon's story parallels Emily and Victoria's. Both relationships begin as adversarial. Gordon and Victoria are both flawed, angry people, who are doing what they can to fix a system from within (it just takes a while for Victoria to get her priorities straight). Just as Gordon can't fight crime in Gotham without Batman, Victoria can't expose Conrad without help from Emily. But while Gordon is aware of and comes to rely on Batman, Victoria has no idea of Emily's role in bringing Conrad to justice.

However, Batman is a vigilante, whereas Emily is not. Batman's goal is much broader than Emily's; she just wants those who wronged her family to suffer. In some aspects, Emily is a blonde reimagining of Batman, but there's a lot she could stand to learn about justice and forgiveness from the caped crusader.

REVENGE READING
THOMAS HARRIS'S
THE SILENCE OF THE LAMBS

Emily's relationship with the White-Haired Man is based on the relationship between aspiring FBI agent Clarice Starling and convicted serial killer Hannibal Lecter in *The Silence of the Lambs*, an acclaimed 1988 novel that became an Academy Award–winning film, starring Anthony Hopkins and Jodie Foster. "They're both cut from the same cloth," Mike Kelley explained to *Entertainment Weekly*. "They're mortal adversaries, but they have a respect for each other, and it's a really interesting relationship."

In *The Silence of the Lambs*, Starling is tasked with interviewing Lecter in order to catch another serial killer: Buffalo Bill. The two develop a begrudging respect for each other. While Lecter never explicitly reveals Bill's identity, he gives Starling cryptic clues throughout their conversations so she can figure it out for herself. This dynamic is reflected in Emily and the White-Haired Man's relationship. He could just kill her, but instead gives her an opportunity to defend herself. He could just tell Emily about her mother, but instead drops hints about who she was. "You must have got that from your mother" is not just a jab at how weak David Clarke was; it suggests that the White-Haired Man knew (and possibly fought) Emily's mother, Kara Wilkins.

When Lecter finally escapes, he doesn't track Starling down. Instead, he sends her a congratulatory note when she graduates from the FBI academy. This is mimicked on *Revenge* when the White-Haired Man lets Emily go free — and even winks at her hidden camera in Conrad's office, acknowledging they are in on a secret together.

Starling has a long, successful career but can never escape Lecter and the impact he had on her life. If Emily chooses to pursue the truth about her family, it's safe to say that Emily hasn't seen the last of the White-Haired Man — and that she better be prepared for a lifetime of looking over her shoulder.

the timeline

With so many plots, flashbacks, and characters involved, it's hard to keep track of what happened when. Below you'll find a timeline of the events that led up to Emily Thorne's arrival in the Hamptons. Where dates are not explicitly established, an estimate is included.

1979 The Stowaway opens.

1981 (APPROX.) Jack Porter is born.

JUNE 1984 Amanda Clarke is born.

SUMMER 1986 Conrad and Victoria get married.

SUMMER 1987 Daniel Grayson is born.

1990 Amanda Clarke's mother, Kara Wilkins, is presumed dead.

LATE 1991 David Clarke buys his Hamptons beach house.

DECEMBER 31, 1991 David Clarke meets Victoria Grayson for the first time.

SUMMER 1992 Grayson Global hosts the annual BBQ by the Beach, and the infamous photo is taken.

JUNE 4, 1993 Flight 197 crashes.

AUGUST 1993 Victoria and Conrad meet with the American Initiative to plan the cover-up.

AUGUST 1993 David Clarke is arrested.

FALL 1993 Declan Porter is born.

SEPTEMBER 18, 1993 Dr. Michelle Banks commits Amanda Clarke to a juvenile facility.

SPRING 1994 Charlotte Grayson is born.

MARCH–JUNE 1995 The David Clarke trial takes place.

JUNE 9, 1995 David Clarke is convicted of treason.

SUMMER 1995 The Graysons found Victims United Outreach.

FALL 1995 Leo Treadwell researches his book about David Clarke.

SUMMER 1996 *The Society Connection* by Mason Treadwell is published.

FEBRUARY 19, 2002 Emily Thorne is arrested and brought to Allenwood.

APRIL 22, 2002 David Clarke dies.

APRIL 24, 2002 Carole Miller walks out of Grayson Global and assumes the name Carole Thomas.

JUNE 2002 Amanda Clarke turns 18 and is released from Allenwood.

DECEMBER 31, 2002 The Graysons host a New Year's Eve party, and Amanda Clarke serves it as a cater waiter.

LATE 2003 OR EARLY 2004 Emily Thorne is released from Allenwood, and Amanda Clarke assumes Emily's identity.

SPRING 2005 Amanda Clarke, as Emily Thorne, spends a semester in Barcelona, Spain.

MEMORIAL DAY WEEKEND, 2011 Amanda Clarke, as Emily Thorne, arrives in the Hamptons.

sources

AfterElton.com.

Albee, Edward. *Who's Afraid of Virginia Woolf?* New York: Signet, 2006.

Andreeva, Nellie. "Pilot Season: The Rise of Feature Directors," Deadline.com. February 27, 2011.

Angelo, Megan. "A Taste for Tidbits Best Served Cold," NYTimes .com. January 12, 2012.

"Ashley Madekwe Covers 'Bello' Magazine's Entertainment Section!," JustJared.com. May 27, 2012.

Atkinson, Nathalie. "Dressing for spying, and *Revenge*," Arts .NationalPost.com. March 7, 2012.

Ausiello, Michael. "Emily VanCamp confirms 'Brothers & Sisters' exit: 'Rebecca has run her course'," EW.com. June 30, 2010.

_____. "Emily VanCamp on Losing *Everwood*, Gaining *Brothers & Sisters*," TVGuide.com. February 2, 2007.

Batman Begins. DVD. Warner, 2005.

Begum, Mumtaj. "Enter the Dark Side," *The Star Online*. ecentral.my. May 6, 2012.

Bentley, Jean. "Connor Paolo Talks 'Revenge' and Being the Dan Humphrey of the Hamptons," AOLTV.com. September 21, 2011.

Bernstein, Abbie. "Interview: Madeleine Stowe gets a taste of *Revenge*," AssignmentX.com. October 26, 2011.

Bibel, Sarah, "'Revenge' Cast Reveal Their Favorite Scenes," Xfinity. comcast.com. March 22, 2012.

_____. "*Revenge*'s Nick Wechsler: Jack is a Huge Threat to Emily," Xfinity.comcast.com. October 26, 2011.

Blake, William. *The Marriage of Heaven and Hell*. New York: Dover Publications, 1994.

Bricker, Tierney. "*Revenge* Creator: '[Spoiler Alert] Will Never Kiss!' But Guess Which Love Triangle Is So On?," EOnline.com. February 29, 2012.

Christie, Agatha. *And Then There Were None*. New York: St. Martin's, 2004.

Chui, Delphine. "Ashley Madekwe talks about her style blog, wedding plans and how Kate Moss inspired her character in *Revenge*," GraziaDaily.co.uk. June 22, 2012.

"Composer Interview: iZLER," Film Music Media. youtube.com/ FMMFilmMusicMedia. May 2, 2012.

Conrad, Joseph. *The Secret Sharer*. New York: Bedford Books, 1997.

The Count of Monte Cristo. DVD. Touchstone Home Entertainment, 2003.

Diamond, Jamie. "Henry Czerny, Reluctant Bad Guy," NYTimes.com. August 21, 1994.

Dumas, Alexandre. *The Count of Monte Cristo*. Trans. Robin Buss. New York: Penguin Books, 1996.

"Emily VanCamp Says Her New TV Character Will Be 'Taking Pleasure' in Executing Revenge," BuzzSugar.com. September 21, 2011.

"Emmys: Mike Kelley, Creator of 'Revenge'," Deadline.com. June 3, 2012.

Euripides. *Medea*. New York: Dover Publications, 1993.

"Executive Producer Series: Marty Bowen," ContentAsia Summit 2011. youtube.com/ContentAsiaSummit. April 1, 2012.

EW.com.

Facebook.com.

Feldman, Dana. "iZLER interview: composer scores hit ABC series 'Revenge'," Beatweek.com. April 6, 2012.

Fitzgerald, F. Scott. *The Great Gatsby*. New York: Penguin Books, 1974.

Franklin, Nancy. "That Seventies Show," NewYorker.com. June 9, 2008.

Frederick, Brittany. "Q&A: 'Revenge' Star Christa B. Allen," StarPulse .com. November 2, 2011.

"From Coast to Coast, Connor Paolo Talks Jumping from *Gossip Girl* to *Revenge*," TheTVAddict.com. August 10, 2011.

Gelman, Vlada. "*Revenge*'s Nick Wechsler Previews the Show's Hot Triangle and Talks Life Post-*Roswell*," TVLine.com. September 28, 2011.

Gonzalez, Sandra. "'Revenge' star Connor Paolo talks tonight's uncomfortable dinner with the Graysons, explains Declan's accent," EW.com. November 2, 2011.

Gordon, Jillian. "Princess of Primetime, Emily VanCamp," *Saturday Night Magazine*. SNMag.com.

Gray, Emma. "ABC's 'Revenge': Why Women Can't Get Enough of This Melodrama," HuffingtonPost.com. April 18, 2012.

Halterman, Jim. "Ashton Holmes Reveals More Kisses Cut From 'Revenge' and What Tyler Truly Wants," AfterElton.com. November 17, 2011.

_____. "Madeleine Stowe, Gabriel Mann, and Nick Wechsler are Out For 'Revenge'," AfterElton.com. April 16, 2012.

_____. "More on the 'Revenge' Cut Kiss, the Emily/Victoria Bitchfest and 'The Nolan'," AfterElton.com. November 16, 2011.

_____. "'Revenge' at TCAs: Gabriel Mann on Tyler Smooches & Being Game for Anything," AfterElton.com. January 13, 2012.

"The Hamptons Beach Houses on the TV Show 'Revenge'," HookedonHouses.com. October 3, 2011.

Harris, Bill. "Tupper believed in 'Revenge'," TorontoSun.com. April 16, 2012.

Harris, Thomas. *The Silence of the Lambs*. New York: St. Martin's, 1998.

"Henry Czerny From ABC's 'Revenge' [interview]," 98.3 The Key
    . keyw.com. September 20, 2011.

Hidek, Jeff. "'Revenge' brought 'Necessary Roughness' star Marc Blucas
    back to Southport," StarNewsOnline.com. September 10, 2011.
    _____. "Stars of 'Revenge' and 'Hart of Dixie' share memories
    of Wilmington," StarNewsOnline.com. September 21, 2011.

Highsmith, Patricia. *The Talented Mr. Ripley*. New York: WW Norton:
    2008.

Holden, Carly. "*Revenge* Actress Emily VanCamp on the Show's Cast:
    'It's Almost Pathetic How Well We Get Along'," VanityFair.com.
    April 17, 2012.

Homer. *Odyssey*. Trans. Robert Fagles. New York: Penguin Classics,
    2003.

Hughes, Sarah. "There's no soft soap from this new avenger,"
    Independant.co.uk. May 28, 2012.

Iannacci, Elio. "Canadian Emily VanCamp is becoming prime time's
    favourite vigilante," Macleans.ca. April 24, 2012.

Idato, Michael. "Malice in Wonderland," SMH.com.au. February 12, 2012.

IMDb.com.

"Indiantelevision.com's interview with *Revenge* executive producer
    Marty Bowen," IndianTelevision.com. December 15, 2011.

"Interview: Christa B. Allen (Charlotte Grayson) from *Revenge*,"
    TheTVChick.com. November 2, 2011.

"Interview: Gabriel Mann (Nolan) teases a *Revenge* Finale Cliffhanger
    'O.M.G.!'," TheTVChick.com. May 2, 2012.

Lacob, Jace. "'Revenge': Emily VanCamp, Mike Kelley, Madeleine
    Stowe, and Gabriel Mann on the ABC Soap," TheDailyBeast.com.
    February 28, 2012.

Larrson, Stieg. *The Girl with the Dragon Tattoo*. New York: Penguin, 2011.

Letizia, Anthony. "*Revenge* and *The Count of Monte Cristo*," Alterna-TV
    .com. February 29, 2012.

LinkedIn.com.

MacKenzie, Carina Adly. "'Revenge' star Joshua Bowman sways us to Team Daniel," Blog.Zap2It.com. October 19, 2011.

Marcil, Monique. "Emily Thorne from 'Revenge'," Blog.Zap2It.com. November 22, 2011.

_____. "Victoria Grayson from 'Revenge'," Blog.Zap2It .com. December 20, 2011.

Marsi, Steve. "Emily VanCamp Confirms, Discusses *Brothers & Sisters* Exit," TVFanatic.com. June 30, 2010.

Masters, Megan. "*Revenge* Boss Teases 'Very Big' and 'Terrible' Things Ahead! Plus: Someone's Leaving!" TVLine.com. January 4, 2012.

Melville, Herman. *Moby-Dick*. New York: Oxford Paperbacks, 2008.

"Mike Kelley: *Revenge*," *The Treatment*. KCRW.com/TheTreatment. May 9, 2012.

Miller, Frank and David Mazzucchelli with Richmond Lewis. *Batman: Year One*. New York: DC Comics, 1988.

Milton, John. *Paradise Lost*. New York: Penguin Classics, 2003.

Murfett, Andrew. "Behind the scenes with *Revenge*," Stuff.co.nz. July 6, 2012.

_____. "Dishing the Dirt," TheAge.com.au. June 7, 2012.

_____. "Q&A with Emily VanCamp," SMH.com.au. June 4, 2012.

Nededog, Jethro. "'Revenge' EP Mike Kelley Reveals 10 Things to Expect Post-Tyler," HollywoodReporter.com. January 11, 2012.

_____. "*Revenge*'s Henry Czerny Teases Conrad's Challenges and the Finale," HollywoodReporter.com. May 16, 2012.

_____. "'Revenge' Star Emily VanCamp on Her New Series: 'There's Quite a Few Takedowns' (Video)," HollywoodReporter.com. September 21, 2011.

"Off the Cuff: Emily VanCamp on Embracing Her Dark Side on 'Revenge'," RollingStone.com. May 30, 2012.

"On the Score: iZLER ('Revenge' on ABC)," Guitar Viol. youtube. com/GuitarViols. October 11, 2011.

Orwell, George. *1984*. London: Penguin UK, 2008.

Pennacchio, George. "'Revenge' actors Nick Wechsler, Gabriel Mann almost quit acting," *Hollywood Wrap*. ABCLocal.go.com. April 25, 2012.

Phillips, Marci. Original interview, via telephone. August 25, 2012.

Porter, Ryan. "Exclusive Q&A with Emily VanCamp," Flare.com. January 31, 2012.

"Queen Victoria: Inspiration," TheMistressOfTheRobes.blogspot.ca. March 16, 2012.

Radish, Christina. "Producer Wyck Godfrey Talks *Goliath*, ABC's *Revenge*, Nicholas Sparks Adaptation *Safe Haven*; Reveals Taylor Lautner Passed on *Goliath*," Collider.com. November 4, 2011.

Rae, Jessica. "Exclusive Interview: Gabriel Mann (*Revenge*) dishes on the Shamu cam, those sideways glances, and more," SmallScreenScoop.com. April 25, 2012.

Rentilly, J. "The Girl You'll Fall in Love with Tonight," MensHealth .com. October 21, 2011.

"Retro best served cold," SMH.com.au. February 9, 2012.

Revenge. TV series. Executive Producers Michael Kelley, Marty Bowen, Wyck Godrey. ABC. 2011–.

Revenge.ABC.com.

RevengeFan.com.

"*Revenge* Stars Dish on Season Finale," *Good Morning America*. May 15, 2012.

Rizzo, Monica. "Emily VanCamp: I Was Desperate for *Revenge*," People.com. October 12, 2011.

Ryan, Maureen. "Your Burning 'Revenge' Questions Answered by Creator Mike Kelley," AOLTV.com. December 11, 2011.

Schipp, Debbie. "Exclusive interview with *Revenge* star Madeleine Stowe by the *Sunday Telegraph*'s Debbie Schipp," DailyTelegraph. com.au. March 4, 2012.

Shakespeare, William. *Hamlet*. New York: Oxford Paperbacks, 2008.

Shelley, Mary. *Frankenstein*. New York: Oxford University Press, 1998.

Shen, Maxine. "Grudge city: 'Revenge' never ends on Hamptons soap," NYPost.com. November 12, 2011.

Shia Ong, Lie. "Q&A With Connor Paolo of ABC's 'Revenge'," MSNTV.com.

Singer, Michael. *A Cut Above: 50 Film Directors Talk About Their Craft.* New York: Lone Eagle, 1998.

"Song Detective Interrogates: Music Supervisor Season Kent," SongDetective.com. April 20, 2011.

SparkNotes.com.

Stanhope, Kate. "*Revenge* Boss on Daniel's 'Dark Turns,' Victoria's Dangerous Blast From the Past, a Time Jump," TVGuide.com. February 28, 2012.

_____. "*Revenge* Cast Shares Six Teases for the Season Finale: 'Every Character is Tested'," TVGuide.com. May 22, 2012.

Steinberg, Jacques. "Take My Wife. Please. I'll Take Yours," NYTimes .com. May 11, 2008.

Stevenson, Robert Louis. *The Strange Case of Dr. Jekyll and Mr. Hyde.* New York: Dover Publications, 1991.

Stransky, Tanner. "'Revenge' boss teases season finale and poses a juicy query: 'Is Emily willing to kill?'," EW.com. May 23, 2012.

"Sync/Master: The Pains of Being Pure at Heart," IndieMusicFilter. com. March 4, 2009.

Szklarski, Cassandra. "Film star Henry Czerny dives into TV with prime time soap 'Revenge'," 680News.com. September 20, 2011.

TelevisionWithoutPity.com.

Tinkham, Chris. "Margarita Levieva: An interview with *Adventureland's* Lisa P.," UndertheRadarmag.com. April 8, 2009.

TomandLorenzo.com.

Trachta, Ali. "Interview: *Swingtown* Creator Mike Kelley," Chicagoist .com. June 12, 2008.

TV.com.

"The TV Addict Interviews Emily VanCamp," TheTVAddict.com. April 18, 2007.

TVFanatic.com.

TVTropes.org.

VanityFair.com.

Villarreal, Yvonne. "Love draws Madeleine Stowe to seek 'Revenge'," LATimes.com. Match 11, 2012.

Wai Ting, Loong. "*Revenge*, just a fantasy," NST.com.my. May 6, 2012.

Webb Mitovich, Matt. "Emily VanCamp on *Revenge*'s Fall Finale, a 'Scary Story,' the Proposal and More: 'Things Get Sticky!'" TVLine .com. December 11, 2011.

Webber, Stephanie. "Interview: *Revenge*'s Nick Wechsler Details on Everything From Script Surprises to Where Jack Is Headed!," Ology.com. November 10, 2011.

_____. "'Revenge' Exclusive: Gabriel Mann, Ashley Madekwe Reveal 7 'Chaos' Spoilers," Ology.com. February 15, 2012.

_____. "'Revenge' Exclusive: Margarita Levieva Dishes on Her 'Amanda Clarke' Character," Ology.com. December 7, 2011.

"What Drives Madeline Stowe Up the Wall?," EW.com. February 4, 1994.

Wieselman, Jared. "Ashton Holmes: I Love Playing the Bad Guy," TheInsider.com. November 16, 2011.

Wikipedia.org.

Wilkes, Neil. "Q&A: 'Beautiful Life' exec Mike Kelley," DigitalSpy.ca. September 15, 2009.

"Will Emily Soon Find an Unexpected Ally in Charlotte Grayson? We Dish on All Things *Revenge* with Star Christa B. Allen," TheTVAddict.com. November 2, 2011.

Zoller Seitz, Matt. "'Revenge' is a dish that serves itself in bits and pieces," Salon.com. September 21, 2011.

acknowledgments

First and foremost, I need to thank my aunt Dorothy and my cousin Erica, whose breathless "I love *Revenge*" comments at Christmas turned me onto a show I probably would have overlooked.

Thanks to Crissy Boylan for editing this book and for putting up with emails that contained too many exclamation marks, unnecessary capitalization, and endless references to Nolan's wardrobe. No editor should be put through that. Thanks to Jen Knoch, a wonderful proofreader, advice-giver, and friend. How I've published two books at the place of your employment and still email you nearly every day perpetually astounds me. Thanks to the rest of the ECW Crew — Jack, David, Erin, Sarah, Jenna, Alexis, Troy, Rachel, Carolyn, & Michael — for letting me invade your world with my bad jokes, gossipy emails, and last-minute proposals.

Thanks to Matt for naming this book (the secret's out, you may now take credit), dealing with all my technical difficulties (and there were many!), and for seeing me at my most insane and choosing to stay.

To Mom, Dad, Jill, & Anne — you guys are the best. As Victoria Grayson says, "Blood is always thicker than water." Which means I can request the following: please buy several copies of this book so I can continue to pay my rent. That's what families are for, right?

GET THE EBOOK FREE
* PROOF OF PURCHASE REQUIRED

At ECW Press, we want you to enjoy this book in whatever format you like, whenever you like. Leave your print book at home and take the eBook to go! Purchase the print edition and receive the eBook free. Just send an email to ebook@ecwpress.com and include:

- the book title
- the name of the store where you purchased it
- your receipt number
- your preference of file type: PDF or ePub?

A real person will respond to your email with your eBook attached. And thanks for supporting an independently owned publisher with your purchase!